Harry Craufuird Thomson

The Outgoing Turk

Impressions of a Journey Through the Western Balkans

Harry Craufuird Thomson

The Outgoing Turk
Impressions of a Journey Through the Western Balkans

ISBN/EAN: 9783744798358

Printed in Europe, USA, Canada, Australia, Japan

Cover: Foto ©Andreas Hilbeck / pixelio.de

More available books at **www.hansebooks.com**

SERAJEVO IN TURKISH TIMES.
From a water-colour belonging to Miss Irby.

[*Frontispiece.*

THE OUTGOING TURK

IMPRESSIONS OF A JOURNEY
THROUGH THE WESTERN BALKANS

BY

H. C. THOMSON

AUTHOR OF "THE CHITRAL CAMPAIGN"

WITH SEVENTY-SIX ILLUSTRATIONS FROM PHOTOGRAPHS
TAKEN BY THE AUTHOR AND OTHERS
AND THREE MAPS

NEW YORK
D. APPLETON AND COMPANY
1897

The Sultan Selim inscribed upon the door of his Palace at Adrianople, these words :—

" O ye, who come here for judgment ; if justice be not done to you, I absolve you from your allegiance to me."

" A cruel tyranny, bathed in the blood of their Emperors on every succession ; a heap of vassals and slaves ; no nobles, no gentlemen, no freemen, no inheritance of land, no stirp of ancient families ; a people that is without natural affection, and, as the Scripture saith, that ' regardeth not the desires of women ' ; and without piety or care towards their children, without morality, without letters, arts, or sciences ; that can scarce measure an acre of land or an hour of the day ; base and sluttish in buildings, diets, and the like ; and, in a word, a very reproach of human society ; and yet this nation hath made the garden of the world a wilderness, for that, as is truly said concerning the Turks, where Ottoman's horse sets his foot people will come up very thin."

Francis Bacon.

PREFACE

I have called this book "The Outgoing Turk," using "Turk" not in the sense of "Mahommedan," but in that of "Osmanli official"; for in Bosnia and the Hercegovina a third of the people are still Mahommedans, protected in all their rights, and with full liberty to worship without insult and without restraint. These Provinces have not been annexed by Austria. They have only been occupied by her for the enforcement of order. Nominally they still form part of Turkey, and are under the sovereignty of the Sultan; but the Pashas, and Turkish officials, "one and all, bag and baggage," have been cleared out, and the government is entirely in Austrian hands. There are many who would have preferred the formation of a tributary State like Bulgaria, but the conditions were not parallel. In Bulgaria there were comparatively few Mahommedans, and hardly any Catholics, whereas in Bosnia and the Hercegovina almost one half of the population was Moslem, and of the Christians a considerable proportion were Roman Catholics. The people were not fit for liberty. They could never have united to form one nation, and to them the gift of liberty would have been but a prolonging of misery. What they were in immediate need of was a strong, firm government, such as Austria has given them. The proclamation announcing the occupation undertook that all the people in the land should enjoy equal rights before the law, and that they should be protected in life, in belief, in property, and in estate. This undertaking Austria has kept. She has established peace where there was never-ending strife. She has evolved government and order out of anarchy and chaos; and under her rule all races and all religions are not only tolerated but protected. A Catholic country herself—an ardently Catholic country—she is making no attempt to favour the Catholics at the expense of either the Turks, or of the Orthodox Christians. She supports and subscribes to the maintenance of them all, though she has treated the Turks with rather more consideration than the others, not only from reasons of political expediency, but from a wise and generous desire to soften the pain of submission, and the bitter sting of defeat.

What Herr v. Kallay, who for the last ten years

has been virtually the Dictator of the two Provinces, has done to develop their resources, and to stimulate their paralysed energies into fresh life, has been fully dwelt upon by other writers; and is too well known to require further comment.

What I have attempted to describe is rather the machinery of the Government; those details which attract so little attention, but upon which a successful administration so greatly depends.

I travelled last summer through Bosnia and the Hercegovina, by carriage and post-cart, more than eight hundred miles, not along the main lines of communication, but through the outlying mountainous districts, far removed from the line of rail, and seldom visited, except by officials during their periodic tours of inspection. The people have been disarmed, and owing to that, and to the excellent system of gendarmerie, perfect security prevails throughout the land. The peasants, it is true, are poor and backward; that is only to be expected, after the centuries of oppression they have had to endure; but every effort is being made to improve their condition, and to lighten their lot. Everywhere I went I found that the resolute yet kindly rule of Baron Appel and Baron Kutschera had produced a wholesome effect. The people feel that their complaints will be patiently listened to, and that justice will not be denied them. Moslem and Christian are beginning to mix with each other on equal terms ; to learn a mutual respect, and a mutual toleration ; and as their embittered feuds die out, the free intermingling of all its peoples to which the land has been so long a stranger, and without which progress is impossible, will become more permanent and more intimate. But wise and humane as the rule of Austria has been, the people are nevertheless discontented : the Turks because they have been deprived of power, the Catholics because they have been given less than they expected, and the Serbs because they desire independence. However well a people may be *governed*, so long as they do not govern themselves there will always be found some to whom a perilous liberty seems preferable to a prosperous servitude. The Orthodox, too, are suspicious of any interference in church affairs, and have resented bitterly a recent order that a government official shall be present at all church councils. They regard it as an attempt to secularise their church, and it has in consequence been productive of intense dissatisfaction. The Greeks in Cyprus have the same sensitive jealousy of interference in church matters. This question of religion underlies everything, and makes it almost impossible for an occupation by any Power that is not Orthodox to ever become acceptable to an Orthodox population.

I have used the expression, "through the Western Balkans," to describe my journey, because the people, alike in Bosnia, in the Hercegovina, in Dalmatia and in Montenegro, call their hills, not as we do on our maps, the Junian, Illyrian or Dinaric Alps, but simply, "The Balkans," the Turkish word for forest-covered mountains.

To write words from another language in such a way as to convey any idea of their pronunciation is a difficult matter; and I have thought it best to adhere to the recognised Croat spelling, but for the benefit of those who may wish to know how the words really sound, I have given a list of geographical names with their phonetic equivalents.

I have to express my grateful thanks to Miss Irby for the invaluable help she has given me, and for the photograph of Serajevo in Turkish times, taken from a water colour drawing in her possession.

I am also indebted to Captain v. Roth of the Austrian Cavalry, whom I accompanied on one of his official tours, and who has a wide knowledge of the country, and of the customs of the people, for much useful information, and for kindly allowing me to use some of his photographs to supplement those I took myself.

Where I have had occasion to quote from the Koran, I have made use of Sale's translation; and for the details of certain Mahommedan ceremonies

I have had recourse to the Rev. T. P. Hughes' *Notes on Muhammedanism*.

About Bosnia itself, the people and their ways, there is little to tell that has not already been fully told by Mr. Arthur Evans. The main object I have had in view has been to show how great a transformation can be effected by twenty years of resolute Christian government in a country in the terrible condition Mr. Evans has so eloquently described.

The pity of it is, that, but for the selfish jealousies of the Powers, what has been done in Bosnia might have been also done in Macedonia.

H. C. T.

TABLE OF GEOGRAPHICAL NAMES USED IN THIS BOOK

Croat spelling.	Phonetic equivalent.	Croat spelling.	Phonetic equivalent.
Banjaluka	Banialuka.	Jajce	Yaitze.
Bihać	Bihatch.	Jezero	Yezero.
Bjelašnica	Bielashnitza.	Konjica	Konyitza.
Bjelina	Bielina.	Metković	Metkovitch.
Blagaj	Blagay.	Marica	Maritza.
Bočac	Bochatz.	Miljačka	Milyachka.
Brčka	Brchka.	Orašje	Orashye.
Bugojno	Bugoyno.	Prjedor	Priedor.
Čarčija	Charchiga.	Ripać	Ripach.
Doboj	Doboy.	Rogelj	Rogegl.
Gacko	Gatzko.	Šamac	Shamatz.
Gornji-Šeher	Gorni-Shahr.	Serajevo	Serayevo.
Gradačac	Gradashatz.	Sokolac	Sokolatz.
Hadžići	Hadzhichi.	Trebinje	Trebinye.
Hercegovina	Hertzegovina.	Treskavica	Treskavitza.
Ilidže	Ilidzhi.	Zenica	Zenitza.
Jablanica	Yablanitza.		

Croat letter.	Approximate sound.
ć	tch
č	ch
c	tz
j	y
G	gl as in Italian.
š	sh
ž	zjh

CONTENTS

CHAPTER I

STATE OF BOSNIA BEFORE THE OCCUPATION—ITS PRESENT CONDITION AS COMPARED WITH OTHER PARTS OF EUROPEAN TURKEY—JOURNEY THROUGH RUMELIA IN 1895 1

CHAPTER II

PERFECT TRANQUILLITY OF BOSNIA AND THE HERCEGOVINA UNDER AUSTRIAN RULE—STATISTICS OF CRIMES OF VIOLENCE—COLONEL CVJETIĆANIN AND THE GENDARME CORPS—DEATH OF BARONESS APPEL—CHANGED FEELING OF THE PEOPLE 11

CHAPTER III

THE PEAK OF TREBEVIĆ—THE OBSERVATORY ON THE BJELAŠNICA—FOREST EXPLOITATION AT RADOVA—THE HOT SPRINGS OF ILIDŻE 18

CHAPTER IV

CORPUS CHRISTI DAY IN SERAJEVO—THE ANNIVERSARY OF THE BATTLE OF KOSSOVO—THE ČARČIJA OR BAZAAR—THE VAKUF SYSTEM—ORDINARY TENURE OF LAND—A BOSNIAN EVICTION—INCREASE OF POPULATION—SPANISH JEWS 29

CHAPTER V

A MURDER TRIAL IN SERAJEVO—CONSTITUTION OF THE COURTS—QUESTIONS BETWEEN MAHOMMEDANS DECIDED BY CADIS—MEKTEBS, OR PRIMARY SCHOOLS—MADRASAS, OR SCHOOLS FOR THEOLOGICAL STUDENTS—THE SCHERIAT, OR FINAL SCHOOL 45

CHAPTER VI

HADJIA STAKA—GIRLS' SCHOOLS IN BOSNIA—ORPHANAGE FOUNDED IN SERAJEVO BY MISS MACKENZIE AND MISS IRBY—A MAHOMMEDAN MARRIAGE—CONDITION OF MAHOMMEDAN WOMEN—BOSNIAN MORALITY 59

CHAPTER VII

THE HERCEGOVINA—THE DEFILES OF THE NARENTA—KONJICA—JABLANICA—SKETCH OF THE HISTORY OF BOSNIA AND THE HERCEGOVINA 78

CHAPTER VIII

THE VALLEY OF THE RAMA—MOSTAR—METKOVIC—SEBENICO—CAVES UNDER MOUNT TROGLAV—FROM SINJ TO LIVNO BY THE VAGUNJ PASS—POLITICAL ASPIRATIONS OF THE CROATS AND SERBS 90

CHAPTER IX

ZENICA—DERVENT—PRJEDOR—NATIVE RACES—POULTRY FARM—DISAPPEARANCE OF TRADE BETWEEN ENGLAND AND BOSNIA 105

CHAPTER X

BANJALUKA—TURKISH BATHS AT GORNJI-ŠEHER—VALLEY OF THE VERBANJE—KOTOR VAROŠ 116

CHAPTER XI

JAJCE—FALLS OF THE PLIVA—SIMILARITY OF CUSTOMS BETWEEN THE MAHOMMEDANS AND THE CHRISTIANS—RELIGIOUS CONSTANCY OF THE RAYAHS 129

CHAPTER XII

JEZERO—VARCAR VAKUF—KLJUČ—THE BRAVSKA PLANINA—PETROVAC—BIHAĆ—TURKISH TREATMENT OF ANIMALS . 141

CHAPTER XIII

GRADUAL RELAXATION IN BOSNIA OF THE STRICTNESS OF MAHOMMEDANISM—DIFFICULTY FOR A MAHOMMEDAN TO SUCCEED IN BUSINESS—DEVICES FOR OBTAINING INTEREST — BIHAĆ — KRUPA — NOVI — TRAPPIST MONASTERY—HOT SPRINGS OF SLATINA—PRVNJAVOR—KARA-VLACHI—DERVENT 155

CHAPTER XIV

FERTILE PLAINS OF THE POSAVINA—ŠAMAC—GRADAČAC—ORAŠJE—THE TOBACCO PLANTATION AND GIRL LABOUR—BRČKA AND THE PRESERVED PLUM INDUSTRY—BJELINA THE SALT SPRINGS OF TUZLA—LIGNITE SEAMS OF THE MAJEVICA—LIFE OF AUSTRIAN OFFICIALS COMPARED WITH THAT OF OFFICIALS IN INDIA 174

CHAPTER XV

JOURNEY THROUGH THE HERCEGOVINA—DRIVE FROM MOSTAR TO RAGUSA—NEVESINJE — GACKO — INTERVIEW WITH BOGDAN SIMONIĆ—BILEK—TREBINJE — RAGUSA—CATTARO—SLAVONIA AND THE MILITARY FRONTIER . . . 191

CONTENTS

CHAPTER XVI

REVIEW OF ENGLISH POLICY IN THE BALKANS 208

CHAPTER XVII

A MAHOMMEDAN VIEW OF THE ARMENIAN MASSACRES AND OF ENGLISH INTERVENTION—HOW THE SULTAN COMES TO BE CALIPH OF ISLAM—PRESENT CONDITION OF MACEDONIA 221

CHAPTER XVIII

INEXPEDIENCY OF ISOLATED INTERVENTION ON BEHALF OF ARMENIA—DOES THE RETENTION OF CYPRUS AFFECT THE PRESENT SITUATION IN CONSTANTINOPLE? 238

CHAPTER XIX

PROBABILITY OF REVOLT IN MACEDONIA—IS ENGLAND'S ATTITUDE TO IT TO BE ONE OF SYMPATHY OR OF DISCOURAGEMENT? 254

CHAPTER XX

IMPOSSIBILITY OF THE TURKS REFORMING, OR OF CESSATION OF MASSACRE—CHANGE OF ATTITUDE OF THE EUROPEAN POWERS—PROBABLE MOTIVES OF RUSSIA—THE NATURAL ALLY OF ENGLAND IS AUSTRIA—ADVISABILITY OF STRENGTHENING BOTH SERBIA AND GREECE . . . 266

ILLUSTRATIONS

	PAGE
SERAJEVO IN TURKISH TIMES . . . . *Frontispiece*	
BOSNIAN MAHOMMEDAN	1
THE NARENTA, NEAR JABLANICA IN THE HERCEGOVINA . .	5
MODERN SERAJEVO	13
THE DEFILES OF THE MILJAČKA. A REGIMENT ON THE MARCH TO PLEVLJE.	19
THE MILJAČKA NEAR ITS JUNCTION WITH THE BOSNA . .	21
BJELAŠNICA	23
THE ČARČIJA, SERAJEVO	25
THE CALL TO PRAYER	30
THE BEGOVA DJAMIA, SERAJEVO . . . . *To face*	32
THE ČARČIJA, SERAJEVO	33
THE ČARČIJA, SERAJEVO	35
TURKISH COFFEE-HOUSE ON THE MILJAČKA	37
SPANISH JEWESS	43
JEWISH CEMETERY, SERAJEVO	46
MODERN SERAJEVO . . . . *To face*	48
CADI	57
CATHOLIC GIRL	61
AN UNMARRIED TURKISH GIRL FROM SERAJEVO	64
TURKISH GIRL	67
TURKISH FAMILY	69
THE ČARČIJA, SERAJEVO	71
UNMARRIED TURKISH GIRL FROM MOSTAR	73
ORTHODOX SERB	74

ILLUSTRATIONS

	PAGE
MOSTAR	79
KONJICA, HERCEGOVINA	81
MOSTAR	83
ALBANIANS	84
THE VALLEY OF THE RAMA	91
THE RAMA VALLEY. HORSES TREADING OUT CORN	92
THE OLD BRIDGE, MOSTAR	93
SEBENICO, DALMATIA . . . . *To face*	96
DALMATIAN COAST, NEAR RAGUSA	97
SOURCE OF THE CETINA	99
FALLS OF THE KERKA . . . . *To face*	100
RACES AT PRJEDOR. PROCESSION OF MINSTRELS WITH WINNING HORSE	106
TURK RIDING WITH CHILD BEHIND HIM	107
FOOT-RACE, PRJEDOR	109
JUMPING ON INFLATED GOAT-SKIN	110
RACES AT PRJEDOR	111
VRANDUK . . . . *To face*	112
BANJALUKA	117
GORNJI-ŠEHER	118
BOSNIAN MAHOMMEDAN	123
SELLING BREAD IN THE ČARČIJA	125
BOSNIAN PEASANT HUT	127
JAJCE	135
CATHOLIC PEASANTS, JAJCE	139
TURK SELLING COFFEE BY THE ROADSIDE	143
KLJUČ, THE ANCIENT CLISSA	145
JABLANICA, HERCEGOVINA	148
SERAJEVO	153
TURKISH HÁN, RAMA VALLEY	161
WOMAN SPINNING AS SHE WALKS	163
MAHOMMEDAN TOMB NEAR BANJALUKA	166
KARA-VLACHI	172
THE CART IN WHICH WE TRAVELLED	173
SLAVONIAN PEASANTS	175

ILLUSTRATIONS

	PAGE
ŠAMAC	177
ŠAMAC	178
POSAVINA PEASANT WOMAN	179
BRČKA	183
MILLS ON THE SAVE	185
BETWEEN TREBINJE AND RAGUSA	192
MOSTAR	193
HERCEGOVINIAN WOMEN	195
BOGDAN SIMONIĆ	196
MONTENEGRIN	197
WOMAN FROM NEAR BILEK	198
THE SOURCE OF THE OMBLA	199
FORT AT ENTRANCE OF THE BOCCHE DI CATTARO	200
CATTARO	201
STAGNO, DALMATIA	202
ZUPANJE	203
SLAVONIAN PEASANT WOMEN	205
SLAVONIAN VILLAGE	207

MAPS

BOSNIA	*To face*	1
PART OF A MAP PUBLISHED IN PARIS IN 1696	,,	204
MAP PUBLISHED IN LONDON IN 1725	,,	206

MAP OF BOSNIA.

THE OUTGOING TURK

CHAPTER I

STATE OF BOSNIA BEFORE THE OCCUPATION—ITS PRESENT CONDITION AS COMPARED WITH OTHER PARTS OF EUROPEAN TURKEY—JOURNEY THROUGH RUMELIA IN 1895

IT is recorded in the Saxon Chronicle that in the reign of King Stephen every man did, not only that which was right in his own eyes, but that which of his natural conscience he knew to be wrong; an accurate description of the state of affairs in Bosnia and the Hercegovina before they were occupied by Austria in 1878.

A little pamphlet describing the condition of the Christian inhabitants, written in German, and published in 1856, begins with these words: "The misrule existing in the whole of the Turkish Empire is so great and so universal, that it can be best characterised as a state of chaotic anarchy. One province, however, and that perhaps the least known of all, has in this respect a sad pre-eminence. It is a province where one can travel only with the greatest difficulty, and with not less danger than in the wilds of Kurdistan; where the intolerance and hate against the Christians is more living and active than around fanatical Damascus; where the insolence of the Aghas is more arrogant than was ever that of the Egyptian Mamelukes; and where the condition of the subject people is more abject and hopeless than that of the fellaheen upon the Nile; that Province is Bosnia."

To any one travelling in Bosnia at the present time, who has not studied its past history, these words must seem a mere foolish exaggeration, so great is the change which has been effected.

Miss Irby, however, who passed through it with Miss Muir Mackenzie as far back as 1862, and who, since 1871, had been living in Serajevo, looking after the orphanage for Serb children, which had been started there through the efforts of Miss Mackenzie and herself, and who therefore knew the country thoroughly, wrote, as late as 1877, that "the devastation committed in Bosnia is unreported and unknown. But I have seen enough from personal experience in quiet times, in both provinces, to appreciate the full truth of Dr. Sandwith's assertion that the usual condition of Bosnia is far worse than that of Bulgaria." And Dr. Sandwith himself, when distributing relief to the Bosnian refugees in Serbia, amongst other terrible stories, told one which brings vividly before the mind the miserable life of the rayah (the name by which the Christian peasant is known all through the Balkans) with its daily possibilities of unprovoked and unpunished outrage. "One woman there was who seemed to have been petrified into a misanthropist. She had no tear to shed, and with difficulty her story was told. She, and her husband, a small farmer, had but one beautiful boy; he was left in their cottage while the two went to work in the fields; they returned at midday, and found their beautiful child lying on the floor dead, and frightfully mutilated. A band of marauding Turks had passed by, and left such traces of their track. A few minutes afterwards the husband had disappeared. In a frenzy of wrath he had seized his axe, and had gone to seek vengeance and death, and has not since been heard of. Most of the families had fled at the first alarm, and had at all events saved their lives. But with such stories as the above I could fill your pages. They had all a horrible sameness about them."

As I sit writing at Jablanica, in the very heart of Bosnia, in a district that was once one of the most fanatical in the country, on the line of railway, with all the comforts and most of the luxuries of civilisation around me, it is difficult to realise that less than twenty years ago the people, whom I now see living in the most absolute tranquillity, were liable to the same sudden frenzies of massacre that have devastated Crete, and at this very moment are devastating Armenia. For Bosnia is now practically a European country, with a network of excellent roads, and with a railway connection between most of the principal towns; and my wanderings through it this summer show that travelling there is not only easy, but that it is perfectly safe. I had been in Turkey, and was amazed at the difference between the two countries. Everywhere in Turkey trade is discouraged, and every obstacle placed in the way of strangers who may be passing through. Moreover the habitual brigandage, and the occasional outbreaks of fanatical violence, render travelling as perilous as it is unpleasant. And apart from the danger, the mere physical discomfort is often very great, as this account of a journey I was obliged to take from Vienna to Constantinople, in February 1895, will suffice to show. The weather was bitterly cold, and the ground covered with snow. We arrived late at night at Mustapha Pasha, the frontier station between Rumelia and Bulgaria, and were told that the Marica was in flood, and the bridge over it broken down; but that it was being repaired, and that most probably we should go on early the next morning.

Mustapha Pasha is a miserable wayside station, with a wretched waiting-room, in which there was a small stove which gave out scarcely any warmth. Till our arrival there we had not felt the cold, as the engine supplied hot air to the carriages, but when the train was stopped the engine fire was not kept

THE NARENTA, NEAR JABLANICA IN THE HERCEGOVINA.

up, and the cold in the carriages that night was intense. It would have been easy to have telegraphed the state of affairs to Philippopolis, so that we might have waited there in comfort, but the railway people had not troubled themselves to do this. We started at daybreak for the Marica, which is some six miles from the station. When we got there we found that no attempt had been made to repair the bridge; and though a train was waiting on the other side of the river, the station-master refused to allow us to cross as a gale was blowing, and he was afraid the caiques would upset. We were therefore taken slowly back to Mustapha Pasha. The carriages of the train into which we had been changed were not warmed in any way, and we suffered greatly from the cold, the ladies especially. Any one who knows what a winter in the Balkans is like will appreciate what we endured. When we reached the station once more we were told it might be two or three days before the bridge could be mended—God knew when—the Turkish officials did not. There was but little to eat or drink, and not much fire to warm ourselves by, and the prospect of remaining there for several days was more than depressing. Fortunately amongst us was a Christian employé of the Porte, who was anxious to return to Constantinople without delay, as his leave had almost expired, and who, being a man of some influence, was able to arrange with the Turkish authorities that those of us who wished to do so, might drive with him across the mountains to Adrianople—about twelve miles—under charge of a guard of zaptiehs, as a protection against the brigands. Needless to say, we all eagerly accepted this means of escape. It was a lovely sunny day, and in spite of the cutting wind we had a really enjoyable drive, though the carriages stuck once or twice in the snowdrifts. But when we reached Adrianople we found that all the three rivers upon which it is built—the Tunja, the Ardha, and the Marica—were rising rapidly, and it was with considerable difficulty that we got into the town at all. As we crossed the Ardha the water was running like a mill-sluice over the top of the coping, and came up as high as the axles of the wheels. Every moment we thought the carriages must upset; but they all got safely over. Had we arrived an hour later we could not possibly have crossed, and would have had to return to Mustapha Pasha in the dark—a difficult and dangerous business—and have waited there till the bridge was repaired, which, as we heard afterwards, was not done for another five days. We slept that night at Adrianople in a fairly comfortable hotel, but the next morning we found to our dismay that the Tunja, which flows between the railway station and the central part of the town, had risen so rapidly during the night that the bridge over it was under water, and all communication with the station cut off. We tried to induce the boatmen to take us over, but they had received orders from the Pasha, the Governor of Adrianople, not to take any one across without his permission. This, after some delay, we managed to obtain, and were landed on the other side without any mishap, but only to find ourselves a mile from the station, on the edge of a swamp, over which the river was rising rapidly. We stood for a moment gazing at it, "like exiles to Siberia," as a Greek lady said with a forlorn attempt at gaiety; but there was no help for it, so in we plunged. We had to crash through a layer of ice, often up to our knees in the freezing water, the cold of which was indescribable, as a bitter wind was blowing, which made it worse; but the ladies struggled bravely on, though one of them, a little Italian woman, kept lamenting volubly that she had ever left her beloved Italy for such a detestable country. At last we arrived at the station, wet through, and hardly able to stand, so benumbed were we with the cold. The train was gone, and there was no prospect of another till the following morning. The people at the hotel were not expecting us, and had no fires ready, so we had to take off our dripping things, and wait between the blankets for the arrival of our baggage, and a change of raiment, "Il faut être des sans-culottes pour l' occasion," as a Frenchman, who shared my room, remarked. The next day we started once more, to be delayed again by another bridge over the Marica, also broken down by the swollen river. Fortunately this time we were able to cross upon planks, laid down from buttress to buttress of the broken bridge. It was a trying ordeal, crossing a roaring torrent, at a height of thirty or forty feet, upon a couple of narrow planks with nothing to hold on by, and it was surprising how well the ladies accomplished it. I think they had gone through so much misery and discomfort, and were so anxious to be at home, that this seemed to them a small matter. The train was waiting on the other side, and there was no choice but to cross; so they did it without stopping to think about it; but I am sure that under ordinary circumstances none of us would have cared to attempt it. Of course the conditions were exceptional, but in any other country some effort would have been made to cope with them. Horses might have been sent down to take us through the swamp, and help might have been given in a number of other ways; but in Turkey there is nothing but apathy and want of enterprise. There is no initiative amongst the people, and no desire amongst the officials to foster trade, or to induce foreigners to come into the country. Indeed, they would be glad to keep them out altogether if they dared, for they dread the feeling of restless dissatisfaction, which an increase of knowledge, and of civilisation, is sure to produce in the minds of the rayahs. Not only must every one have a passport, but it must be viséd by the Turkish authorities in the traveller's country, and is only good for the town named in the visé. Those who wish subsequently to visit any other part of the Turkish dominions, or even Egypt, must obtain a teshkaré, or permit from the Sultan, to do so. The Customs regulations, too, are most irritating. All luggage is strictly scrutinised, not only to see whether it contains any dutiable article, but whether there is in it any book or writing, criticising or commenting in any way upon the religion of Islam, or upon the Ottoman Government. At Mustapha Pasha, where our luggage was examined, the Customs officers seized one of my books because the word "Constantinople" occurred on the top of one of the pages. They said it must be sent to Constantinople for perusal, and that if it were found to contain nothing objectionable, I could have it back by applying at the Custom House there. As I was leaving for Alexandria directly after my arrival, I had no time to do this, and so lost a book I valued exceedingly. I was better off, however, than my French fellow-traveller, who had twenty-three books seized, simply because they were written in French, a language the officials were unable to understand. They were perhaps unusually strict at the time, for the Armenian massacres were beginning, and the Christians all through Rumelia were in a state of feverish excitement. Several people had been killed that week in the streets of Constantinople, and there was everywhere a general feeling of apprehension that the Turks might rise at any moment, and that the terrible scenes of the Bulgarian massacres might be repeated in Rumelia, as, since then, they have been in Constantinople itself. I have never before realised how awful it must be to live under an ever-present dread of impending massacre.

CHAPTER II

PERFECT TRANQUILLITY OF BOSNIA AND THE HERCEGOVINA UNDER AUSTRIAN RULE—STATISTICS OF CRIMES OF VIOLENCE—COLONEL CVJETIĆANIN AND THE GENDARME CORPS—DEATH OF BARONESS APPEL—CHANGED FEELING OF THE PEOPLE

DURING my journey this summer through Bosnia and the Hercegovina, I found everything very different from the state of things I have been describing. All around me I saw comfort and energy and order. There was none of the listless unconcern, the slipshod decay, that prevails throughout Turkey, where no buildings are kept in repair, or even in decent cleanliness. The Turks are still " base and sluttish in buildings," as Bacon said of them centuries ago; unchanged, and unchangeable, in that as in everything else. The towns have a repulsive appearance of squalor, with garbage lying about in the open streets, and the buildings crumbling gradually to pieces. In Bosnia, on the other hand, the towns are now full of new and handsome houses, and factories are springing up, bringing with them wealth, and an increase of comfort. The streets, even the bazaars, are kept scrupulously clean by a sanitary department, which inspects rigorously all the sellers of milk, fruit, and other perishable articles. In short, the country, externally, has become civilised, and the people are correspondingly happier and more prosperous.

There are two routes to Bosnia from Vienna, one through Agram, the capital of Croatia, the other through Buda-Pesth. That through Agram is the more direct, but I decided, on account of the better train service, to go by Buda-Pesth, which city I left on the afternoon of the 2nd June, reaching Brod in Slavonia at eleven that night. There the train crosses the Save to the town on the opposite bank of the river,—Bosna-Brod, as it is called—where the Bosnian railway begins. Nearly all the names of places in Bosnia have a meaning describing their physical characteristics. Brod, for instance, means "ford." Before the opening of the railways destroyed the river traffic, it used to be one of the most important towns on the Save. Now it is of little consequence. A police sergeant was inspecting passports at the station, but when I explained that mine was in my portmanteau, he politely said it would be sufficient if I would give him my card. The same thing occurred on my arrival in Serajevo; and only once during my stay in Bosnia was the production of my passport insisted on. Nothing could exemplify in a more striking way the changed times. How completely Bosnia, formerly so remote and inaccessible, has been brought into touch with the rest of Europe, may be gathered from the fact that it is possible to be in London in fifty-four hours from the time of leaving Serajevo; the train, which starts from there at five in the evening, reaching Vienna the following evening in time to catch the Ostend express.

Herr von Horowitz, of the Bosnian Department in Vienna, had kindly given me a letter of introduction to Baron Kutschera, the head of the Civil Administration of Bosnia and the Hercegovina, and on my presenting it I met with a very cordial welcome. Indeed, all the time I was in Bosnia I received every-

STREET IN MODERN SERAJEVO.

where the greatest possible kindness and help. The Government desire to open the country out as fully and as speedily as possible, and any one who may wish to travel through it, may feel sure of receiving both courteous treatment and assistance; and the land is in itself so interesting and so beautiful, that as the knowledge of this, and of its absolute security becomes more widely known, more people will be attracted to it; though the old idea of the difficulties, and even of the danger, of a journey through Bosnia, and still more through the blood-stained Hercegovina, is hard to dispel.

The most convincing proof of the tranquillity that prevails is furnished by the statistics of the crimes of violence committed in the two provinces, during the last three years, which I have at present before me. In 1893, six men and one woman were condemned to long terms of imprisonment for murder, and one man for highway robbery. In 1894 one man was executed, and four men and one woman were sentenced to imprisonment for murder, there being no cases of robbery with violence. In 1895, no one was executed, but four men and two women were imprisoned for murder, and four men for robbery. And this in a country where formerly brigandage and murder were crimes of daily occurrence. Which of the European states, with a population of a million and a half, can show greater security than this?

While I was in Serajevo I had the pleasure of making the acquaintance of Colonel Cvjetićanin, the commandant of the excellent gendarme corps which has been mainly instrumental in bringing this state of things about. He shared in the stiff fighting that took place in 1878; and, when the campaign was over, entered the gendarmerie, and during the abortive rebellion of 1882, organised a flying column, which, by the rapidity of its movements, effectually crushed out the brigandage, which at that time was so rife. The corps now consists of 2,000 men, drawn from all parts of the Austrian Empire, and of 500 Turks. They are well paid and well pensioned, so a good class of men are induced to join, though the discipline is severe, and any breach of duty is followed by stern and instant punishment. That is absolutely necessary when dealing with men in whose hands so much power must perforce be placed. Gendarme posts, holding eight or ten men under the command of a wachtmeister or sergeant, are dotted all over the country, but especially on the frontiers, and it is owing to the grip they have of it that so small a garrison is necessary. The duties the men are called upon to perform are various : they patrol the district, investigate cases of crime, and give assistance in any emergency that may arise. They are expected to see to the sick in outbreaks of epidemic disease, until medical aid can be procured ; to teach the peasants how to recognise and deal with blight ; and, in short, to be, as one of their officers laughingly said to me, general maids of all work. There is a wholesome regulation that they must work in couples, so that one shall act as a check upon the other, opportunities for oppression or extortion being thereby minimised. The peasants seem to like them, and to appeal to them in all sorts of petty squabbles: "God is God," they say, "and what the gendarme says is holy."

Consul Holmes, in his despatch of 1871, gives a trenchant description of the police whom this gendarme corps has replaced. "The Turkish police," he writes, "is, with much justice, a subject of grievance. A great many of the men are notoriously bad characters, who generally have to bribe the Colonel and Binbashi for admittance to the force, and reimburse themselves by extorting money almost wherever and whenever employed." It is pleasant to compare the present with the past.

For Austria to reconcile to her sway a proud people who had successfully withstood her attacks for the last 300 years, and who, when handed over to her by their own sovereign the Sultan, were not subdued until after a fierce though brief conflict, has indeed been no easy task; and it speaks volumes for the forbearance and tact shown by the conquerors, that the conquered should ultimately have acquiesced so peacefully in an alien rule. A touching instance of the change of feeling that has taken place occurred soon after my arrival in Serajevo upon the sudden death of the Baroness Appel, the wife of Baron Appel, who, for the last twelve years, has been the Governor of Bosnia. Baron Appel has obtained the regard of all classes of the community, and on his wife's death there was an outburst of emotion, unmistakable, widespread and sincere, which showed how greatly she, too, had made herself beloved. Herr von Kallay, who is Minister for Bosnia as well as Finance Minister for Austria-Hungary, in his telegram of sympathy to Baron Appel, expressed truly the universal feeling when he said, "With us also sorrows—I am sure of it—the whole land of Bosnia and the Hercegovina, for the taking away of an untiring helpmate in the furtherance of your Excellency's various weighty projects, and of a sincere friend of the poor." All over Bosnia I heard the same expression of personal sorrow, a sorrow that at one time would not have been possible. The first few years of the occupation were years of stern, though no doubt of necessary, punishment and repression, and both consideration and kindness have been required to efface the rankling memories of the past. Baroness Appel, by the unfailing sympathy she showed to all classes alike, Christian and Turk, Orthodox and Catholic, had no small share in bringing about this good understanding. I have never witnessed a more impressive scene than the funeral procession which followed her body through the streets of Serajevo; and, indeed, it is no light achievement to have thus won the homage of a humiliated and keenly sensitive nation.

CHAPTER III

THE PEAK OF TREBEVIĆ—THE OBSERVATORY ON THE BJELAŠNICA —FOREST EXPLOITATION AT RADOVA—THE HOT SPRINGS OF ILIDŽE.

SERAJEVO, the Damascus of the North, as it is often called, is situated on the banks of the Miljačka (the "charming"), a little river which well deserves its name. It falls into the Bosna a few miles below the town, and in the summer is only a rippling half-dry brook; but the deep gorge by which it has forced its way through the hills, shows that in the winter and spring it must be a powerful stream. The houses are built upon both banks—nestling close under the hills, which circle round them from the back, while in front lies the fertile and beautiful plain, through which the Bosna flows. On the right the hillsides slope gradually upwards, and are covered with woods and plum gardens; but on the left they rise precipitously and culminate in the conical peak of the Trebević, 5,000 feet in height, up to which I walked one afternoon when the heat of the day was over, reaching the top a little after seven. I found there a rest-house, built by the Tourist Club of Serajevo, where I supped and slept. I was struck with the moderation of the charge. That for the bed, which was comfortable and spotlessly clean, was only sixpence, and the supper was proportionately cheap. In the morning the sun rose in a clear and cloudless sky, and I was able to see across the intervening hills, almost as far as the Montenegrin frontier. On the opposite side of the valley rose the wooded ranges of

THE DEFILES OF THE MILJAČKA. A REGIMENT ON THE MARCH TO PLEVLJE.

the Igman Planina, the Treskavica and the Bjelašnica —the white-topped—the last crowned by a line of snowy peaks, on the highest of which the Government has lately erected an observatory where travellers can be received for the night, to which, being only some thirty miles distant from Serajevo, I subsequently paid a visit. I started by an early train for Ilidže, which I reached at seven o'clock, walking on from there to the Bosna-Vrelo, where the Bosna breaks out from the foot of the hills in twenty or thirty springs, all close together, and flows down into the valley at once a considerable stream. There I arranged with a peasant, a Serb, to guide me as far as Radova, a hamlet situated about half-way to the observatory. We had a stiff climb for the first hour and a half, following the bed of a dry water-course, which comes so straight down the mountain side, that seen from below it looks like a Roman road tilted on end, or the funnel of a fire-escape let down through the surrounding trees. It led us into an extensive pine forest, through which a roughly constructed railway, for the exploitation of the timber, winds circuitously down from Radova to Hadžići, a station on the line to Mostar. The rails are made of wood, and follow the curves of the ravine along the sides of which they are laid. The trees are brought to Radova by earth shoots, and are there sawn into planks, to be sent down to Hadžići, the loaded waggons descending by their own weight, but having to be drawn up again by horses when empty. This forest railway was of much interest to me, as I had seen a somewhat similar but more primitive mode of exploitation in the Himalayas. Mr. MacDonnell, the forest officer in Chamba, had a deodar forest there to exploit, and found it a difficult task to get the deodars down into the river Ravi from the heights upon which they grow. It was not possible to make a railway as here at Radova, for the value of the trees lies in the size of the trunks, which have to be floated down to India entire. He, therefore, arranged a number of earth shoots down which the trees were

THE MILJACKA NEAR ITS JUNCTION WITH THE BOSNA.

shot to the head of a stream a mile and a quarter from the Ravi, along one side of which he constructed a roadway by laying down a succession of trees side by side in fours, with a tree superimposed upon each of the outer ones so as to form a trough-like channel. The inclination was so steep that the trunks attained a velocity of nearly twenty miles an hour in spite of their being slowed down at a half-way station, and the roadway had to be kept constantly wet to diminish the effect of the friction. It terminated abruptly at a cliff fifty feet above the Ravi, where I stood and watched the trees as they came down. It was a wonderful sight. Huge trunks, seventy feet and more in length, came twisting round the corners of the gully, tearing along with a noise like thunder, and hurling themselves at last over the edge of the precipice, standing for a brief moment poised upright in the river bed until they were seized by the current and swept away. When the forest was worked out the roadway was gradually broken up from the top, and the trees of which it was composed shot down one by one until the whole were gone.

At Radova, I found a colony of Tyrolese foresters, and a nice clean little inn. My guide refused to go further, as he did not know the way, and the men being all at work I could not get another. But the people at the inn assured me there was only one path leading to the observatory, and that if I kept to it I should find my way there in time; and that an occasional glimpse through the trees of the snow in the distance, would insure my being in the right direction. In places the wood was very thick and dark, and I strayed several times off the track, which in places was very faintly defined, but I managed to find it again, and finally emerged upon a lovely upland meadow, covered with grazing cattle, and close under the snowy peak on which the observatory stands. There I found some Serb peasants herding their flocks.

We smoked a cigarette together, and they showed me where the path re-entered the forest. The ascent then became steeper, and I suffered intensely from thirst. I had not come across a brook or a spring since leaving Radova, and I was glad to moisten my lips with a little snow. I discovered afterwards that this scarcity of water is a distinguishing feature of all the Bosnian mountains. On the other side of the wood I met some peasants coming down with laden pack-horses, and by raising my hand to my mouth I was able to make them understand what I was in need of. One of them, pointing with his hand, said "Chesma." This I understood at once, as "chasma" is the Hindustani word for spring, presumably a Persian word introduced by the Mahommedans, both into India and into the Balkans. Here, too, I made my first practical acquaintance with the difficulty which all strangers have of distinguishing between the Christians and the Turks, for they all wear turbans and the same style of dress, which consists of an embroidered waistcoat with a loose open jacket, full trousers

BJELASNICA.

gartered at the knee, a cloth bandage bound tightly round the leg like the Indian puttee, and "opankas," or rough, heelless shoes with turned-up toes. The richer men wear silk gaiters and Austrian shoes, and in the towns many of the Turks wear a fez. Before the occupation there was never any difficulty in discriminating between them, inasmuch as the Christians were forbidden to wear clothes of gay colours, and were obliged to dress in sombre garments, befitting their servile condition. Above all things they were not allowed to wear the Prophet's green, the distinguishing badge of the Mahommedans, and the punishment for infringing this unwritten law was so terrible, that it was seldom broken. These distinctions are now being rapidly obliterated. The Christians are increasing in prosperity, and have equal rights with the Turks; and many of the latter, owing to their disinclination for steady work, are becoming abjectly poor. Still there are many little signs by which those who are used to the people can distinguish at once what a man is; not only if he is a Turk or a Christian, but if he is Catholic or Orthodox. For a stranger it is almost impossible. These peasants were greatly interested in my camera, the object of which they understood perfectly, and amused themselves by looking at different objects in the finder. When we went our respective ways I said "salaam," the Mahommedan salutation, thinking they were Turks; but they replied "Not salaam—sbogom—God be with you—we are not Turks but Serbs." I should explain here that the word Turk as used in Bosnia is altogether misleading. It does not mean a Turk, but a Mahommedan, for of real Turks—Osmanlis—there are scarcely any. These Mahommedans are

THE ČARŠIJA, SERAJEVO.

mostly descended from the old Bosnian nobles, who, being heretical Bogumiles, were bitterly persecuted by the Catholic Church, and who therefore gladly accepted in a body the religion of Islam, when the country was conquered by the Turks in the fifteenth century. To this the abject position of the Bosnian rayahs was in great measure due, for in addition to the humiliations entailed upon them as Christians, which they endured equally with all the other rayahs in the Ottoman Empire, in Bosnia they suffered also from the feudal tyranny which existed there in the most acute form before the Turkish conquest; the Bosnian landlords, even so late as the fifteenth century, regularly exporting their peasants, and selling them as slaves. It is not therefore to be wondered at that the Capitanović, the Kulenović, the Tschengić, and the other great Mahommedan families, who claim an unbroken descent from these Bosnian chieftains, should have looked upon the liberties of their rayahs with the same contemptuous indifference that a feudal lord did upon those of his serfs. But though the position of the peasants was degraded in the extreme, and the wrongs they had to endure were almost indescribable, there were never in Bosnia the organised massacres which have disgraced other parts of Turkey, and even during the insurrection most of the atrocities were committed, not by the Mahommedan Slavs, but by the Osmanli officials, and by the troops sent up from Constantinople.

I reached the observatory a little after six, only to find it enveloped in a thick mist, so that I was deprived of my hoped-for view. The keeper told me the nearest spring was that to which I had been directed by the peasants, and that as it took two hours to fetch water from it, they depended mainly upon the rain-water in their cisterns. It must be a lonely life, though he has with him an assistant, a married man, whose wife looks after the house. In the summer it is not so bad, but in the winter they are not able to go out for weeks together, except to take the necessary observations, and he told me they could often see the noses of the wolves pressed against the window-pane. These beasts are very numerous, and there are also many bears, one of which, not long ago, carried off an ox from the meadow through which I had passed. He told me that a more direct path than that by Radova had been marked out through the forest by the Tourist Club, and that I should have no difficulty in finding it, as the trees had been splashed with red paint at intervals of every few feet, and with these to keep me straight, I found my way down easily enough.

The peak of the Bjelašnica was unfortunately still shrouded in mist when I left it at sunrise, but as I crossed the Igman Planina, the lower range of hills between the Bjelašnica and the valley of the Bosna, the view was superb. The forest here had entirely changed in character, and was no longer composed of pines, but of oaks, beeches, and hazels.

I reached Ilidže at two o'clock, hot and dusty, for it was the middle of June, and a Bosnian sun is a good deal hotter than an English one, and was glad of a bath in the water of the famous hot spring, which when it wells up from the ground has a temperature of 65° Centigrade. By the time it has traversed the pipes to the different bathing establishments, it is considerably cooler, but is still quite hot, and most refreshing in its effects. There have been baths there ever since the time of the Romans, and the water has a great local reputation as a cure for rheumatism and other kindred ailments.

CHAPTER IV

CORPUS CHRISTI DAY IN SERAJEVO—THE ANNIVERSARY OF THE BATTLE OF KOSSOVO—THE ČARĆIJA OR BAZAAR—THE VAKUF SYSTEM—ORDINARY TENURE OF LAND—A BOSNIAN EVICTION—INCREASE OF POPULATION—SPANISH JEWS.

I WAS fortunately still in Serajevo when Corpus Christi day came round; one of the most imposing of the ceremonies of the Catholic Church. In the early morning I lay and listened to the melodious cry of the muezzin, or Hodja, calling the faithful to prayer, and an hour or two later I watched the solemn procession winding through the streets to the pealing of church bells, the tramp of armed men, and the repeated firing of salutes. My mind went back to the days when the Christians were forced to worship by stealth, when no church bells were permitted, when the people had to be called to prayer with a wooden clapper, and when the churches were not allowed a steeple, and might only be small, unpretentious hut-like buildings. I saw one of these old churches afterwards at Samac on the Save, which has been left still standing (though a new church has been built near it), which is not more than twenty feet in height, and could not, I think, hold more than fifty people. In Serajevo, the old Serb church is modestly hidden behind a dead wall, fronting upon the street, with a small door at one side, so that it may not look like a church, and thereby attract attention, and arouse the anger of the true believers. "When the Turks hear the church bells," say the Serbs, "then is their hate against the Christians kindled."

In the book written by Miss Mackenzie and Miss Irby on the Slavonic provinces of Turkey, passage there is a which gives a vivid picture of the abject state in which the Christians lived. "In the poor little church (of Turkish Gradishka), Vaso showed us

THE CALL TO PRAYER.

with pride a bell which the Christians of Gradishka had dared to hang up in accordance with their rights—the only bell in any orthodox church in Bosnia which could be heard from the outside. The Mussulmans would not tolerate the sound. But Vaso boasted that their bell could be heard even across the Save."

Not long after Corpus Christi day I saw an

equally interesting celebration of the Orthodox Church—the anniversary of the battle of Kossovo, that last great fight, on June 15th, 1389, when the life of the Serb nation was extinguished for centuries. It is to every Serb a consecrated day —a day of mourning for the past, but of a never dying aspiration for the future. At Knin, in Dalmatia, in the midst of a Catholic population, are several Serb villages, one of which bears the name of Kossovo. This year more than 10,000 peasants assembled there to celebrate the anniversary of the battle. The Catholic Croats do not share in and have no sympathy with these patriotic rites, for the Orthodox Christians are to them heretics, whom they hate almost as much as they do the Turks. One of them, at Vrlika, told me that his landlord came back from this village of Kossovo, and annoyed him so much by talking about the future of the Serb race, that they had hot words, and he sought a lodging elsewhere.

The religious hatred existing between these Slav peoples, who are one and the same race in language and blood, is greatly to be regretted, but it is idle to hope that it will ever be obliterated, or in any sensible degree lessened. If a common misery could not unite them, it is vain to imagine that now, under happier auspices, any reconciliation can be effected. To the Serbs not only is their Church the one true faith, but to it they anchor their hope of becoming once again a great and powerful nation.

I attended, in Serajevo, a solemn service for the soul of the Serb king, Lazar, who was killed at Kossovo, and in the evening I was present at a Serb concert, where the national music was played, and national songs were sung. Everywhere there was open and undisguised enthusiasm ; the passionate outburst of a crushed and outraged people in the first intoxication of comparative freedom. In the early days of the occupation, the Austrians discouraged these exhibitions of national sentiment, but wiser counsels have prevailed, and they are now allowed freer vent.

Serajevo is a straggling town, with a population of more than 36,000 people, who are the strangest mixture of races and religions. By far the most interesting part is the bazaar, the Čarčija as it is called, which is very similar to the bazaars in the East. It consists of narrow little streets of wooden shops, slightly raised from the ground, in which the proprietors sit cross-legged all day, retiring at night after locking them up, to their respective quarters of the town. The variety is delightful. Proud-looking Mahommedans, fur-coated and caftaned Jews, peasants in their tattered garments, squalid gipsy beggars, Turkish women veiled from head to foot, and pretty, frank-looking Christian maidens in flowing trousers and wooden clogs. In the middle stands the beautiful Begova Djamia, the third finest mosque in Turkey. In the courtyard is the invariable fountain, where the

THE BEGOVA DJAMIA, SERAJEVO

[To face p. 32.

THE BEGOVA DJAMIA

worshippers perform the necessary ablutions imposed by their religion; cleanliness being declared by the Prophet to be one-half of the faith and the key of prayer. By the side of the fountain stands a venerable sycamore tree, planted, so tradition says, by Usref Beg himself, at the time when he founded the mosque. He captured the fortress of

THE CARCIJA, SERAJEVO.

Jajce, obtaining for that achievement the title of Ghazi, or Conqueror of the Infidel; but he is remembered less by his courage than by his piety. He and his wife devoted the greater part of their property to ecclesiastical uses, and founded not only this mosque, but the madrasa which stands near it, the school where Mahommedan youths, destined for the priesthood, are enabled to study free of cost. The mullah, who acts as instructor, kindly translated for me the inscription over the doorway, setting forth that it was built by Ghazi Usref Beg, the Glory of Justice, and the Fountain of Benevolence. In the courtyard of the mosque is a stone exactly a yard in length, or the Turkish equivalent for a yard, to which traders in the bazaar repair, when they have a dispute, in order to ascertain the correct measure. Near it is the little building in which are contained the clocks from which the Hodja calculates the hours for the calls to prayer. All Mahommedans are supposed to worship regularly five times a day. The prayers they use are unvarying; so many times must they lay their foreheads on the ground, repeating as they do so a stated verse of the Koran; so many times must they raise themselves to a sitting posture, with their eyes closed, and with their hands placed upon their knees; so many times must they rise and remain absorbed, while they repeat silently so many prayers; not one prayer or one position must be omitted. It is instructive to notice how all religions tend to stiffen under the influence of a priesthood. No religion in the world is a more empty form than Mahommedanism, and none was originally less so. "It is not righteousness" were the words of its founder, "that ye turn your face in prayer towards the East and the West, but righteousness is of him who believeth in God, and the Last Day, and the

Angels, and the Scriptures, and the Prophets; who giveth money for God's sake unto His kindred, and unto orphans, and the needy, and the stranger."

A great deal of land in Bosnia is Vakuf, or ecclesiastical property, dedicated by the donors to religious and charitable objects, and held in trust for

THE ČARČIJA, SERAJEVO.

the keeping up of mosques, hospitals, schools, fountains, and baths, for looking after the cemeteries, and for giving relief to the sick and the poor. Under the Turks the administration of these dedicated properties had become very corrupt; the incomes were diverted from their legitimate purposes into the pockets of the officials, and everything was in a state of disorganisation and confusion. The Austrian Government has done no more admirable work than in reducing it into order. The whole of the Vakuf properties have been placed under a central department in Serajevo, the administration of which, subject of course to revision by the Government, has been left in the hands of the Mahommedans. That it is well managed is proved by the income having quadrupled itself during the last ten years—that is to say, it has made a steady increase of twenty per cent. each year; its total income being now 300,000 gulden (£25,000). There are rather more than 300 Vakuf tenants or kmets, the greater number of whom are in the neighbourhood of Bihać and Varcar Vakuf. They are better off than any other kmets in Bosnia, because their rents have been fixed by ten yearly contracts, calculated at the rates prevailing at the time when the contracts were made, and as the value of the land is on the increase, they are paying considerably less at the end of the ten years than they would otherwise be doing. The Vakuf administration is also content, inasmuch as the rents are paid regularly and in cash, and they are, therefore, able to make regular payments to the Imams, and Hodjas, whilst formerly they could only pay them with difficulty when the rents were extorted from the kmets.

Part of the income is now expended in improvements; in Turkish times that would never have been thought of. The Secretary of the Vakuf (a Mahommedan) had lately returned from a visit of inspection to the various kmets, and had recommended that two oxen should be given free of charge to each of them. It would cost the administration altogether about six thousand gulden (£500), but it would enable the fields to be better cultivated, and so in time they would produce a larger revenue. Much the same measure was adopted some years

TURKISH COFFEE-HOUSE ON THE MILJAČKA.

ago in the Central Provinces of India, where the Government advanced money to the cultivators for the purchase of seed grain, and of larger oxen to enable them to get rid of a particular kind of grass which was causing great damage, and could only be rooted out by a heavier plough and bigger oxen than those in ordinary use. The Vakuf system is an excellent one; it acts instead of a poor-law system, and now that the administration is so well managed, and can be trusted to dispense its revenues faithfully, the amount of dedications is sure to increase, for with the Mahommedans, as with the Jews, almsgiving is an act of devotion so strongly inculcated as to be almost a matter of obligation. The words of the Koran in which it is enjoined have a strangely familiar ring, and might well have been taken from the Bible :—

"If ye make your alms to appear, it is well, but if you conceal them, and give unto the poor, this will be better for you, and will atone for your sins, and God is well informed of that which ye do." But lest it should be thought that deeds alone would save a man, Mahommed was careful to add that humanity in words and actions is better than alms after injustice.

In 1878 the greatest uncertainty was found to exist with regard to the titles under which land was held. This mischief was remedied by introducing the Austrian system of the Grundbuch, in which are entered the names of all proprietors, and the dates of all sales and mortgages affecting land.

By means of it land can be transferred with the greatest ease and simplicity, at little cost; and a title once registered is incontestable.

For the determination of most questions relating to land, recourse was had to the Turkish Law of Sefer, 14, 1276 (12th September, 1859), a law so favourable to the tenants that it had been allowed to become practically a dead letter.

Several species of tenure are met with, but the most common is the métayer tenancy, under which the landlord or bey takes a definite proportion of the produce of the land in lieu of rent. This proportion varies according to the custom of the district, but as a rule it consists of one-third, and is therefore called the tretina. The cultivator takes the remaining two-thirds, but out of it he has to pay a one-tenth part, called the desetina, to the Government. Formerly the desetina as well as the tretina was paid in kind, but the former is now paid in money, the tretina in most instances being paid, as heretofore, in produce. The landlord is expected to keep the tenant's dwelling house and the farm buildings in repair, and if he wishes to sell, the kmet, and after him the neighbours, have a prior right of purchase, before the property can be transferred to a stranger. This is an excellent provision, as it prevents the land being bought up from spendthrift landlords by rich speculators, and the tenants summarily evicted. The kmet may give up his holding at any time he pleases, but he cannot be evicted except for default in payment of his tretina, or for leaving the land uncultivated, or for doing wilful damage to it. Under the Turks ten years' arrears of rent could be recovered, but the Austrians have reduced the time to one year, after which no arrears can be claimed. This is much more favourable treatment than is accorded to the tenants in most other countries.

Disputes between landlord and tenant as to the amount of the tretina are settled by reference to the desetina, which is always fixed first. The Bosnian Government has done all it can to assist the kmets, and even advances money to them to buy their holdings, in case the landlord should be willing to sell. More than 200,000 kmets have purchased in this way, and are now free proprietors, and the number is constantly increasing. At the census of 1885 there were only 117,000. It is a wise policy, for it is the free peasants who form the mainstay of a country. In the same spirit is conceived the law, that if a man cultivates a piece of waste land, after ten years it becomes his own. The law, too, with regard to evictions, is singularly lenient. A man's dwelling house cannot be seized, and land sufficient for his support must be left him.

An eviction, wherever it occurs, is always a pathetic sight. In Bosnia they are fortunately uncommon; and when they occur, they are generally forcible ejectments of members of a zadruga or joint family. I was present at one of these—of a son who would not work in community with his father and brothers, and who having appropriated some of the joint fields for his own use, the father in self-defence had obtained a decree for his ejectment.

The officer of the court was attended by two

gendarmes, and by a representative of the landlord, of whom the joint family were kmets. He read out the decree before the assembled family, and taking over formal delivery from the son of his share in the joint property, transferred it to the father. Then the son's wife and children, and all his household goods, were brought out from the room he had occupied in the zadruga, and he was told to take them away, as he belonged to the family no longer. It was all done very quietly, though it was painful to listen to the moaning lament kept up by the wife and the children, and to hear the son calling down imprecations from Heaven upon his father, which the old man, who was in no way to blame, and who had borne with him patiently until it was not possible to do so any longer, evidently felt deeply, though he bore it without much outward sign of flinching. I noticed that the son was smoking cigarettes all the time, but smoking in Bosnia is not a luxury; from long habit it has become a necessity, and tobacco is very cheap. Give a Bosnian a cigarette and a cup of coffee, and he will be quite satisfied, however poor he may be, but deprive him of these and he becomes discontented and restless. I heard afterwards that the son had taken up a plot of waste land which he was going to cultivate. It was an instance of the way in which the joint family system, so admirably adapted to the needs of a primitive people, is breaking down under the strain of modern life.

Under the Turks, the manner in which the desetina was collected was terribly oppressive; for the harvest was not allowed to be gathered until the tax collectors had calculated the amount due to them, and there was no appeal from their decisions however iniquitous they might be. Originally, too, the landlords, the beys, and the aghas, were only entitled, like the Government, to a one-tenth share, but they gradually increased this to one-third and even more. Nor did their exactions cease there. What was far worse was the way in which, whenever they felt inclined to do so, they quartered themselves upon their kmets, taking the best of everything, without paying for it, and committing all kinds of excesses and brutalities. The law itself is exceptionally just and fair; it is the way in which it is enforced in Turkish countries that is so mischievous. How awful a tyranny it may become may still be seen in Macedonia, where all the old abuses exist in the most acute form.

The most convincing proof of the increasing prosperity of Bosnia is furnished by the statistics of population. I have not been able to obtain the numbers for 1878, but in 1885 they were as follows:—Total population 1,336,097, of whom 492,700 were Turks, 571,250 Orthodox Christians, 265,788 Catholics, 5,729 Jews, and 630 Protestants and Nazarenes.

In 1895 the census shows that the total population was 1,568,092, of whom 548,632 were Turks, 673,246

Orthodox Christians, 334,142 Catholics, 8,213 Jews, and 3,859 Protestants and Nazarenes. It will be seen that the increase in these ten years since 1886 is as follows:—Of the total population, 231,995, which is made up thus: Turks, 55,932, Orthodox Christians, 101,996, Catholics, 68,354, Jews, 2,484, and 3,229 Protestants and Nazarenes—a noticeable fact is that the total male population is 88,288 in excess of the female, the males being 828,190 in number, and the females only 739,902.

SPANISH JEWESS.

The increase of Jews is to be accounted for by the Jew traders, who have been attracted into the country from Hungary by the increasing opportunities of trade. The Jews who have been in Bosnia for centuries are of quite a different class, and hold rigidly aloof from the newcomers. They are descendants of the Spanish Jews who, when driven out of Spain in 1574, obtained permission from the Sultan, Murad III., to settle in Bosnia and Serbia. They number altogether about 7,000, their headquarters being in Serajevo, where there are no less than 3,000 of them. They still speak Spanish, and have preserved untouched most of their ancient customs and habits. Their burial ground is outside the town on the lower slope of Trebević, and the unhewn boulders forming the tombstones, which have to be very massive in order to keep away the wolves, give it a weirdly impressive look.

·

CHAPTER V

A MURDER TRIAL IN SERAJEVO—CONSTITUTION OF THE COURTS—QUESTIONS BETWEEN MAHOMMEDANS DECIDED BY CADIS—MEKTEBS, OR PRIMARY SCHOOLS—MADRASAS, OR SCHOOLS FOR THEOLOGICAL STUDENTS—THE SHERIAT, OR FINAL SCHOOL

As I expressed a wish to see something of the workings of the law under the new *régime*, I was kindly taken by a friend to hear the trial of a murder case in the district court of Serajevo. Two Turks had agreed to leave Bosnia, and go to some country where they could be under Mahommedan rule. Whenever the Mussulmans are dispossessed of power, the more fanatical of them emigrate, for they are taught that flight is preferable to submission to the infidel. Numbers left Bulgaria when that country was freed, and during the first few years of the occupation many of them left Bosnia also; but now that the first burst of anger has passed away they have ceased to do so, for being Bosnians as well as Mahommedans, it is a terrible trial to them to leave the land which their fathers possessed before ever the Turks came into Europe.

Still even now, in moments of impatient discontent, some go away, but in most cases after a year or two of exile they return, unable to resist the longing for home. Many have come back who had gone to Syria, saying that they are better off in

JEWISH CEMETERY, SERAJEVO.

Bosnia, and so every year the number of those quitting the country is becoming less.

These two Turks, being without passports, were trying to steal into the Sandjak of Novi Bazar. One had money, the other had not. The first night they slept in the woods, near Vishegrad, where the country is very wild. They had with them some raki, the Turkish word for spirits—probably plum brandy, the usual drink in Bosnia—and when night came on they took to drinking to keep up their courage. The story of the accused, who was the one with no money, was that at the last moment he repented of the step he was taking, and declared he would not go; that his companion being enraged by his refusal, attacked him, and that in self-defence he killed him, and that having killed him, he thought he might as well take his money. The theory of the prosecution was that the assassination was solely due to motives of plunder.

The accused put forward four pleas : First, that the act was done in self-defence. This, if proved, would have been a sufficient answer. Secondly, that he was under the influence of drink, and did not know what he was doing. In England drink is no excuse, but in Austria it is always accepted in mitigation of the sentence. Thirdly, that he was subject to epileptic fits. The evidence showed that he had never been known to have fits; that they had not sufficient drink with them for him to have been drunk; and that there was nothing to show that he did the act in self-defence; and in all probability he would have been sentenced to death, had he not advanced the final plea that he was under twenty years of age. This was found to be the case by his recruiting paper, and he was accordingly sentenced to fifteen years' penal servitude, as by the Austrian law no one can be executed who is under twenty. He was tried by five judges, all having an equal vote, the decision being that of the majority. But of these judges three only were official, the other two being assessors, taken from the people. In this instance one was a Serb, the other a Spanish Jew. In India the judge is also assisted by assessors, but he can over-rule their opinion, merely stating what it is, and that he disagrees with it, and his sentence is then confirmed or reversed by the High Court. That is a necessary provision in India, as some of the Hindu sects will not take life; but in Bosnia the assessors have an equal vote with the judges, and, I was told, make a full and unrestrained use of it. The case was opened by a public prosecutor, the accused being defended by an advocate also appointed by the Government; but the whole of the pleadings were in Slavonic. One or two of the witnesses, it is true, gave their evidence in German, but what they said was translated to the prisoner, and the final summing-up of the judge was in Slavonic also. The importance of this cannot be over-rated; it guarantees a fair hearing. The court was crowded with Turks, who followed the evidence point by point. There is nothing so calculated to create confidence in an administration as an open court, whose proceedings are in the national tongue. One of the greatest evils of the Osmanli rule was the use of Turkish in the courts of law, a language unintelligible not only to the Christians, but to nearly all the Mahommedans.

From the District Court an appeal lies to the Supreme Court, but only on points of law. The Supreme Court is composed also of five

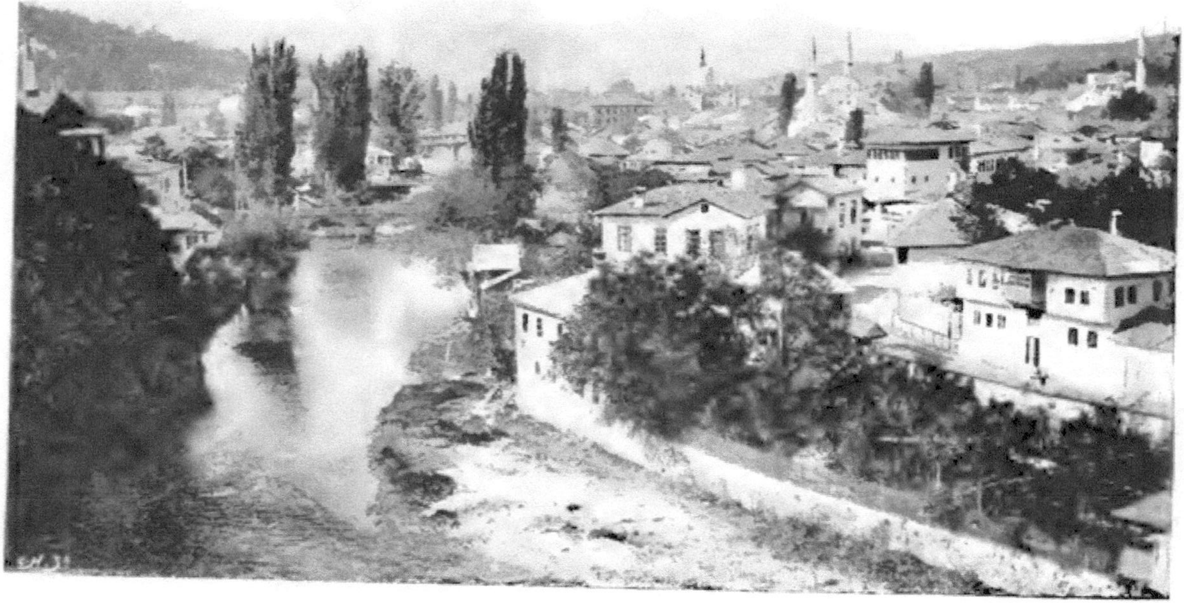

MODERN SERAJEVO.

To face p. 42.

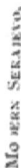

judges, but they are all official judges, none of them being assessors. One of the prominent merits of the present system of law in Bosnia is the fewness of appeals, for it has been truly said that it is better to have a case decided once and for all by the worst possible court, than to have a series of appeals to courts however good. *Summum jus saepe est summa injuria.* It is certainly so in India. There the people are litigious, and will fight a case out to the bitter end, and the right of appeal after appeal is causing the land to pass gradually into the hands of money-lenders and pleaders, who have not the same feeling of pride in it as the sturdy warrior stock who originally owned it, and so an incalculable amount of harm is being done. The English criminal law is excellent in its inflexibility, and in its equal application to all, but many district officers have told me they would gladly see a curtailment of the right of appeal. And a contemplation of the enormous fortunes amassed at the Indian Bar, leads irresistibly to the same conclusion. I know from my own knowledge that in one of the towns of the Punjab, there was lately practising a pleader, not even of the first grade, and a man of no standing whatever, who began life with scarcely anything, but who before his death was the owner of nine villages. The feeling against him became so strong that he was recently assassinated. It is true that by successful ability large fortunes can also be amassed at the

E

English Bar, but the conditions in the two countries are entirely different. The natives of India in many ways are like children, and much greater harm can be done than is done in England, by giving them unrestricted opportunities to squander their wealth in lawsuits. The Indian Government are quite alive to the mischief of this persistent litigation, and have done all they can in the non-regulation provinces to diminish the bad effects produced by it. A decision affecting land cannot, in those provinces, be carried out by the court which has given the decree. It must be sent for execution to the Deputy Commissioner, who summons before him all the creditors of the landowner, and if possible makes an arrangement for his land to be administered in trust for all of them, so that, when they are all paid off, it shall revert to the owner. In this way numbers of old families have been saved from ruin.

The Austrian Government, actuated by the same motive, have wisely limited the number of appeals. The District Courts have a jurisdiction in cases up to 300 guldens, from which there is no appeal whatever. In cases above that amount there is an appeal to the Supreme Court at Serajevo, but in no case is there any appeal to Vienna. In India a case heard before the subordinate judge is appealable first to the district judge, from him to the High Court, and from the High Court to the Privy Council, all at a ruinous expense.

The Austrians have also established an excellent court called the Bagatelle Gericht, or court for trifling causes, in which cases up to fifty guldens are tried, and decided in a summary way, no lawyer being allowed to appear. Moreover, the number of lawyers in the country is strictly limited, and none are admitted to practice until there are vacancies. I am not sure of the number, but I think it is only sixteen for the whole of Bosnia and the Hercegovina. It is a system which has its disadvantages, but on the whole it is better for a people in so backward a state as the Bosnians to run the risk of an occasional miscarriage of justice, than to suffer from a continual fomenting of quarrels by needy pleaders.

It is instructive to compare this reliability of justice with the Turkish system described by Consul Holmes. "Lately the Tijaret Medjliss (Tribunal of Commerce) at Mostar, was suppressed, and all matters referred to the Mekemmeh (Turkish Religious Tribunal). As there are numerous Austrian traders at Mostar, this irregularity was strongly protested against by the Austrian Consul at Mostar, and by the Consul-General here. At Serajevo the greatest confusion prevails. The President of the 'Temiz-i-Houkouk' Medjliss (Court of Appeal), and of the Mekemmeh, is the same person, and matters which ought to be judged by the civil law (the Nizam Nameh) are decided by the religious law (the Sheriat) according to the

Cadi's good pleasure," and he sums up his description with the declaration that all the officials are corrupt. "I do not hesitate to say that of all cases of justice, whether between Mussulmans alone, or Turks and Christians, ninety out of a hundred are settled by bribery alone."

But Mahommedans are in everything a curious contradiction. The Pashas, and the Cadis, and all the governing classes, are hopelessly venal and untrustworthy; and yet the word, and still more the oath, of a Mahommedan who is not an official, may be accepted implicitly. In Aden, for instance, in the English courts in suits between Arabs alone, the defendant is asked if he wishes the plaintiff to be sworn, and if he says "yes," it is held to be an agreement that he will accept the truth of what he says. The plaintiff is thereupon sworn, and a decree is given for the amount he swears to be due to him without any further evidence being adduced. It is not because of the Mahommedan religion, but in spite of it, that corruption reigns all over Turkey. What indeed can be sterner than Mahommed's denunciation? "There is of them who have received the Scriptures, and to whom, if thou trust a talent, he will restore it unto thee, and there is also of them unto whom if thou trust a dinar, he will not restore it unto thee unless thou stand over him continually with great urgency. This they do because they say we are not obliged to keep justice with the heathen, but they utter a lie against God knowingly. Yea, whoso keepeth his covenant, feareth God, and God surely loveth those who fear Him. But they who make merchandise of God's covenant, and of their oaths, for a small price, shall have no part in the next life."

What is bringing about the downfall of the Turkish Empire is the inherent weakness of the Ottoman Government, and its promotion of corruption amongst its officials. The jealousies and hatreds that exist between the surrounding Christian powers would effectually guarantee its continuance if the intolerable abuses of its administration did not lead to uprisings among its Christian subjects, and to savage reprisals by the Turks.

There is much that is excellent, not only in the Mahommedan religion, but in the spirit of the Turkish laws. The canker at the root of them is the absolute power intrusted to the Sultan, who is able to appoint without possibility of question the most unworthy favourite to the highest offices in the state. He is the most absolute autocrat in the world, for under him there are no nobles, all Turks being theoretically equal. They are not even supposed to have a family (I am not speaking of the Bosnians, but of the Osmanlis), and have therefore no family name. They are only spoken of as So-and-So, the son of So-and-So (for example, Osman, the son of Ali), or by some nickname describing some mental or physical peculiarity, some name, for instance, such as the Magnificent, or the Hunchback.

"A heap of vassals and slaves; no nobles, no gentlemen, no freemen, no inheritance of land, no stirp of ancient families."

The Sultan can make or unmake a Pasha at his pleasure; and it is this precarious tenure of their dignity that makes them so corrupt. A Turkish officer, talking to me about the Abyssinian expedition, expressed in a sentence the reason why the Porte has never governed and never will govern properly.

"You gave Lord Napier a peerage, did you not?" he remarked, "and attached to it the payment of a certain yearly sum to maintain it with?"

"Yes," I said, "I believe we did."

"That," he exclaimed, "is where you English are so wise. When a general or an admiral does something worthy of reward, you not only give him a peerage, but you also give him the wherewithal to keep it up. Now with us it is quite different. We make a man a Pasha and give him a province, and he has to make enough during the time he has it to keep himself upon afterwards."

That is one of the chief causes of Turkish misrule.

Austria having undertaken to administer Bosnia in accordance, as far as possible, with the laws she found in existence there, has very rightly maintained the independence of the Turkish courts in all questions in dispute between Turk and Turk: all matters appertaining to marriage, family quarrels and succession to property, being settled by Mahommedan courts, presided over by Mahommedan judges, from whose decisions however, there is an appeal to the Supreme Court at Serajevo, assisted by Mahommedan assessors.

In India it is different. There Mahommedans and Hindus alike are obliged to bring their suits before the ordinary tribunals of the land, in which the judges may be English, or Mahommedan, or Hindu. Great was the horror of one of the Bosnian Turks when I told him that a Mahommedan case might be decided by a Hindu judge; but though the Austrians have been precluded by feelings of honour and good faith from making any more changes than were absolutely necessary, I cannot help thinking that the English system is in the end productive of better results; for in ruling a Mahommedan population it is always well to make them understand from the very outset that they must submit themselves to the laws of the Government under whose authority they have to live, even though it be an infidel Government, and to create in their minds a feeling of confidence in the integrity and impartiality of its tribunals. In India one of the most noticeable facts about our administration is that all creeds unite in their preference for an English judge, and so far from creating friction the obligation to have recourse to our courts is one of the strongest holds we have upon the loyalty of the people. In the early days of the Company suits between Mahommedans used, I am told, to be decided by the Cadis, as they are in Bosnia, but the system was not found to work well, and was therefore abolished. A judge in a Mahommedan case may, however, if he thinks it advisable, send for a Moùlvi, to sit with him in court, not to concur in his judgment in any way, but to assist him on difficult points of law; and in the same way in a Hindu case he may avail himself of the services of a Brahmin Pundit to elucidate any difficult passage in the shastras.

In Bosnia the existence of a special tribunal for themselves, tends to keep the Mahommedans apart, and to retard that gradual process of amalgamation with the rest of the people which is so greatly to be desired. But as, owing to the conditions under which the country was occupied, a drastic change was impossible, no pains have been spared to make the Cadis efficient and reliable. Under the Turks the cleverer boys were drafted from the mektebs, or primary schools, into the madrasas, or theological colleges maintained out of the funds of the Vakuf, or ecclesiastical trust. There they remained for four years, receiving their education and maintenance free of charge; after which they went on to the college for softas, a higher theological college in Constantinople, a resort to which the Austrian Government has now wisely rendered unnecessary by the establishment of a final ecclesiastical and legal school in Serajevo itself, called the scheriat school, the "scheri" being the name of the code of Mahommedan law. In this school the students are put through a long and careful course of instruction with a view to being subsequently taken into the Government service as Cadis. The course is a severe one, comprising not only the Koran, which is of course taught in Arabic, but law, procedure and logic, which are taught in Turkish, and history, geography, and other subjects of general knowledge, which are taught in Slavonic. The Turkish Government did nothing to promote education, but the Vakuf had the administration of a certain number of madrasas and primary schools, where, however, nothing was taught but the Koran. These schools the present Government has not interfered with, but they have done all they can to encourage the Turks to send their children as well to the schools they have established for the use of all classes of the community, irrespective of religion, for very little of any real value can be learnt in the Turkish schools. All they are taught there has to be acquired through the medium of another language—either Arabic, or Turkish—their mother tongue being Slavonic; so that their schooling often consists in the mere listless repetition of phrases conveying but little meaning to the mind. I visited one of the mektebs, and found the children sitting on their heels, with the teacher squatting in front of them, while they repeated in a monotonous sing-song verses from the Koran. Each child was saying a different verse, the result being a confused babel of voices, to which the teacher did not seem to be paying any attention, the children leaving off, and beginning again, apparently just as they pleased. In the madrasas also no general subjects are taught, but the softas, or students, are thoroughly grounded in the Koran. They are maintained for seven years out of the funds of the Vakuf, after which they are qualified to become Hodjas and Imams, and as many of the most promising as there are vacancies for, are transferred, after the fourth year of their course, to the scheriat school, where there is room for thirty pupils. There they stay for five years, undergoing the severe training I have described, in order to be fitted to become Cadis, or Judges.

CHAPTER VI

HADJIA STAKA—GIRLS' SCHOOLS IN BOSNIA—ORPHANAGE FOUNDED IN SERAJEVO BY MISS MACKENZIE AND MISS IRBY—A MAHOMMEDAN MARRIAGE—CONDITION OF MAHOMMEDAN WOMEN—BOSNIAN MORALITY

WHEN Miss Muir Mackenzie and Miss Irby travelled through the country in 1862 there was only one school for Christian girls in the whole of Bosnia and the Hercegovina. In some places they found that the Mahommedan girls were taught to repeat prayers, and to do embroidery, but there was only this one school for Christian girls. It was kept by a woman named Hadjia Staka, the daughter of a Hercegovinian merchant, who was in every way a remarkable woman. As a child she was often made to read the Gospel in church, a great innovation on the usual practice, and as she grew older her father taught her to assist him in his business. In later life she acquired the title of Hadjia, or Pilgrim, because she made a pilgrimage to Jerusalem, and after that she always wore the black garb of a nun. She herself taught reading, writing, and embroidery, and made a journey purposely into Serbia to obtain the services of a properly educated teacher. She used frequently to act as agent between buyer and seller, and was allowed to conduct cases for poor people in the law courts like a regular attorney. In a country like Turkey, where women have no recognised position, this was a very remarkable thing, and is a sufficient proof of her ability.

The two ladies were the more struck by the neglected condition of Bosnia, because in Serbia and in Montenegro there were good schools, while in Bulgaria, which was not then free, the American missionaries of the Robert College were quietly spreading education amongst the people, and were indeed a mighty factor in the preparation of the country for freedom. But in Bosnia there was only this one school; so on their return to England they succeeded in forming an association under the sanction of the Archbishops of Canterbury and York, and of Lord Shaftesbury, for the promotion of education amongst the Slav children of Bosnia. Dr. Norman Macleod, with his usual large-hearted charity, also took an active interest in the matter, and so too did Dean Stanley. The funds raised in England and Scotland were at first entrusted to the Protestant-Deaconess Institution of Kaiserwerth, which made a difficult and arduous beginning in 1869. Two years later Miss Irby went out herself to Serajevo, where she has carried on the work ever since. The Turkish officials made no opposition, looking on a girls' school as a harmless craze quite

SCHOOLS

below their notice. But it took time and patience to convince the rayahs that there was no intention to proselytise or denationalise their children. Every enslaved nation is characterised by deceit and suspicion, and these poor peasants had been so long accustomed to cruelty and injustice that it was not easy to awaken their trust in any disinterested human sympathy, and clinging desperately to their Church as to the ark of their nation, it was but natural that in this new school, opened by Protestants, with foreign customs, and the observ- ances of another Church, they should have sus- pected an intention to Pro- testant- ise their children. When however they found that no attempt was made to influence them against their own Church, but that the declared object of the association was rigidly adhered to, that is to say, to give the girls a practical useful education based upon the doctrine of Christ, and so, not only to effect a gradual elevation of their intellectual and social condition, but to prepare them

CATHOLIC GIRL.

to be the future teachers of their countrywomen, more children were brought than could possibly be taken in, and it was found necessary to restrict the admissions entirely to orphans. Soon after the association began its work the Serb community of Serajevo, under the protection of the Russian Consul, and with money from Russia, set up a school for themselves. The French and Italian Consuls also were able to start a school for the Roman Catholics, under the direction of the sisters of St. Vincent de Paul.

During the insurrection the girls were removed to Prague in Bohemia, while Miss Irby and Miss Johnson, who was then with her, started schools for the fugitives on the Dalmatian and Slavonian frontiers, where they were distributing the relief fund which had been raised in England. After it was over the orphanage was again opened in Serajevo, both for boys and for girls, and many of the children now hold good positions under the Austrian Government.

I will give the story of one of the boys, told me by Miss Irby, as it shows that the same anxious desire for education exists in Bosnia as in Bulgaria, though in a lesser degree. Those who have read the life of Stambuloff will remember the heroic struggles he made to educate himself. This boy's start in life was quite as hard. He was one of the fugitives in Dalmatia, and begged hard to be taken into the school, but as he was clothed and fed by a tradesman who employed him in his shop, his request was refused for some time ; but he entreated so persistently to be accepted that he was finally taken in, and was brought back with the other children to Serajevo when peace was restored. He remained there in the Boys' Home for two years, and was then apprenticed to a trade. But whilst he was working at this he attracted the notice of the master of the gymnasium, who got him a scholarship, and he distinguished himself so greatly that he was ultimately given one of the scholarships to the Vienna University, where he also got on very well. Unfortunately, he died soon after leaving it. I should mention that scholarships may be gained from the Government gymnasia at Serajevo and Mostar to the Universities both of Vienna and Gratz.

I have given the history of Miss Irby's orphanage at some length, not only because it was the first to give an impulse to education in the land, but because it is gratifying to think that England has had some little share in helping the people in their bitter struggle for liberty. And though the conditions of life in Bosnia are now happily altered, the orphanage is still as greatly needed as ever ; for the true idea of a training school reaches indeed far beyond the mere equipment for school examinations.

It is when they are over, and the home quitted that friendly support is often as greatly needed as it is difficult to render for the girl teacher sent forth to sink or swim in the miry waters of Eastern

Europe. It is this support that the orphanage tries to give. In a less extensive way it is, in fact, doing the same kind of work that the Robert College does in Rumelia and in Bulgaria.

While I was in Serajevo I was kindly taken by a friend into one of the Mahommedan courts, and whilst I was there a Turk presented himself to be married. The bride was not present at all, but was represented by a male relative, who took his place before the Cadi with the bride- groom and two male wit- nesses. In this case both the witnesses were men, but it is permissible to have one male and two female witnesses; a woman in Mahommedan law being only equivalent to half a man. The ceremony is of so purely civil a charac- ter, that it must not be per- formed in a mosque, but nevertheless it has infused into it a good deal of religious sentiment. It is not a mere legal formality like marriage before a registrar. The procedure was this. The Cadi first drew up the marriage contract, and inserted in it the amount agreed upon for dower. The bride- groom and the bride's attorney then came in front

AN UNMARRIED TURKISH GIRL
FROM SERAJEVO.

of him, with the witnesses standing on either side. All who were present knelt reverently down, and recited the creed or profession of belief; after which the bride's attorney, taking the hand of the bridegroom, asked him if he consented to the marriage, and to the amount of the dower mentioned in the marriage contract; to which the bridegroom replied that he did. In this case the people were poor and the dower was only ten guldens, about seventeen shillings; but some dower, however small, must always be given. The Cadi then prayed that God would grant that there might be the same mutual affection between the newly-married couple as between Adam and Eve, between Abraham and Sarah, between Moses and Zipporah, and between Mahomed and Ayesha. That completed the binding part of the ceremony, but in Bosnia, just as in India, there are afterwards marriage festivities, which in the case of wealthy people are exceedingly costly. The reason why some amount is always fixed for dower, is that it may act as a check to the facility of divorce which in Mahommedan law is a matter that rests entirely with the husband. He can divorce his wife at once, and absolutely, by repeating three times the words "Thou art divorced;" but in that case the wife is entitled not only to her dower, but to all the property she herself brought to her husband. A wife can also obtain a divorce for ill treatment, but to do so must forfeit her dower.

A Mahommedan may legitimately have four wives, but in Bosnia it is unusual for him to have more than one. Nor is the marriage so entirely a matter of arrangement as in most eastern countries. The courtship of the heart plays an important part in Bosnian poetry (much of which is really beautiful), and enters largely into the lives and habits of the people; so much so, that in almost all the Mahommedan houses a slit is made in the outer wall of the courtyard, which is the recognised place where lovers may converse. As children play together, and girls are unveiled until they are married, there are ample opportunities for falling in love, and if the parents withhold their consent, an elopement is deemed to be quite allowable, no disgrace attaching to the couple on that account. But when once married, a woman's life is one of absolute seclusion. She is immured in a harem, and scarcely ever goes out: when she does so, she must envelope herself in a long cloak called a feredje, which covers her from head to foot, and a yashmak, or veil, to conceal her face. In Constantinople and in Egypt an aperture is left in the yashmak for the eyes; but in Bosnia not only does it completely cover the face, but not unfrequently a kind of mask is worn over it as well. Even the hands are not supposed to be seen. It is pitiable to watch the married women fumbling along by the side of a wall, feeling their way with pushed-out hands covered over with their cloaks. Awkward and ungainly, indeed, is the figure they present,

CONDITION OF MAHOMMEDAN WOMEN 67

waddling along with loose shoes that flap against the ground, and down at heel white stockings. When I was in Serajevo I was in the habit of having my coffee and cigarette at the Cafe Binbashi, a charming Turkish garden on the banks of the Miljačka. Immediately below it is the place where the women gather to do the household washing. They were generally Serbs, but amongst them I occasionally saw a bevy of Turkish damsels standing in the shallow water, with uncovered heads and bare arms, chattering gaily in all the enjoyment of the fresh air, and of the invigorating exercise of beating the clothes upon the stones. It was saddening to think they were destined to so sorrowful an imprisonment as marriage would bring to them. I have spoken to ladies who have been in the harems, and who

TURKISH GIRL.

have received visits from the wives of the richer Begs, and they all say it is impossible to keep up any sort of friendship with the inmates; they have no ideas in common, for as children the Turkish women are utterly uneducated, and after marriage their vision is bounded by the sky, and by the four walls of the courtyard. They are seldom, they say, ill-treated, and they often exercise great influence over their husbands and sons; an influence that, under the circumstances, can only be for evil; to drag them down rather than to help them up. It was, I think, the Caliph Omar who said, ask a woman her advice, and do the contrary; and brought up as the women are, his opinion is hardly to be wondered at. In Turkey proper, and in Egypt, the seclusion is not so strict as in parts of Bosnia, but in India it is even stricter. There the women, after marriage, never go outside the house at all. In both countries those of the lower classes are obliged to do so, and unveiled. They have to work in the fields, and when a man approaches, they merely hide their faces in their garments; but in India, directly a man is able to do so, he secludes his women, putting them, as it is called, behind a purdah or curtain; it is a sign of greater respectability. I had an Afghan servant in Peshawur who asked me if he might build a bamboo screen around the door of his house (one of the servant's houses in the compound), so that his wife might have a little fresh air without being seen. He did not speak of her as his wife, but as his mother. Once when one of his children was teething, and cried continually, I asked if I might get it a coral. "I will ask my mother," he said, and came back with the answer that the child might have it, if it were one that no Christian child had used.

I was told by a friend, a forest officer, that when going over to Pangi, a remote valley in the Himalayas, at the back of the native State of Chamba, he took with him a servant from the Punjab, who had been married just before they started, They had to cross the Sach Pass, which is 14,000 feet high, and covered with snow. Part of the way they had to glissade down, and in other places there was some rather stiff scrambling, and he was curious to know how the wife had got across, for he had seen nothing of her. He asked the husband how his *household*

TURKISH FAMILY.

was, and was told that *it* was well; and he heard afterwards that the poor little woman had been shut up in a kilta, the wicker basket in which the Kashmiris carry baggage, and had been taken over the pass in it upon a man's back. One of the strangest sights in India, and one which throws a strong light on the feelings of the people, is the way in which women are taken upon railway journeys. If a man is not rich, his wife merely covers herself in a specially thick garment, and sits motionless by his side. I travelled once from Lahore to Multan in the hot weather. In the carriage with me was a Mahommedan official who had been transferred to another district, and who had his wife with him. For four hours she sat under the stifling folds of her garment, without speaking a word and scarcely even moving, and without being once given a drink of water, though her lord and master, and myself, were glad to slake our thirst at every station we came to. He simply took no notice of her, any more than if she had been a portmanteau. The wife of a man of higher position is taken about in what to us seems a very comical way. A kind of cupboard is formed by retainers, who carry screens in front and at the side, in the middle of which the woman walks; a way is cleared through the crowded platform, and the cupboard is brought right up to an engaged carriage, the blinds of which are closely drawn, and the door of which stands ready open; she jumps quickly in, closely veiled, and it is shut again before any one has had even a glimpse of her.

In Bosnia there are contradictions. There is a fanatical seclusion of the women, and in places there is an unusual freedom. At Jablanica, for instance, and all through the valley of the Rama, I found the Mahommedan women working in the fields quite unveiled, nor did they make any attempt to hide their faces as I passed them. The explanation I was given was that the Mahommedans around Jablanica are descended from the old Bogumile families, who had their headquarters there, and who, when they accepted Islamism, never quite gave up their attachment to their old faith, traces of which are said to linger still amongst them. But there are signs everywhere that the diffusion of knowledge is

THE ČARŠIJA, SERAJEVO.

gradually breaking down in Bosnia, as it is in India, the rigid severity of the old ways. Many of the Begs will now allow their women to be treated by a doctor when ill, sometimes even by a man doctor, though to be doctored at all is contrary to the fatalism of their belief. Moreover, the more enlightened Mahommedans, who reflect thoughtfully upon their own religion, must be aware that the Prophet obviously did not intend that women should be immured so strictly as they have been. All that the Koran says is this: "Oh, Prophet, speak unto thy wives, and thy daughters, and the wives of the true believers, that they cast their outer garments over them when they walk abroad. This will be more proper that they may be known to be matrons of reputation, and may not be affronted by unseemly words or actions." It was an injunction meant as a protest against the licentious behaviour of the Arabs. A study of his life, and of the Koran, shows that Mahommed never intended women to be reduced to the nonentities they have since become. His own wives played a prominent part in his life, and in reality, both by his teaching and by his conduct, he endeavoured to raise women into a higher position than they had hitherto held amongst the Arabian tribes. There is a popular fallacy that the Mahommedan religion denies that women have souls, or that they will rise again; a fallacy which has arisen partly from the degraded position they hold in all Mohammedan countries, and partly from the fact that they are not allowed to enter the mosque at the same time as the men. There are, however, certain hours allotted to them when they may go there to pray. It is, indeed, quite a mistaken idea that Mahommed denied to them the hope of Paradise, but it is a calumny that has been so often uttered against him, and the religion he founded, that I will give his exact words. They are to be found in chapter xxxiii. of the Koran: "Verily the Moslems of either sex, and the true believers of either sex, and the devout men, and the devout women, and the men of veracity, and the women of veracity, and the patient men, and the patient women, and the humble men, and the humble women, and the almsgivers of either sex, and the men who fast, and the women who fast, and the chaste men and the chaste women, and those of either sex who remember God frequently, for them hath God prepared forgiveness, and a great reward."

In Turkey, women do not work in the fields, as they do in most semi-civilised countries, or rather Christian women do not, for fear of being subjected to insult from any passing Turk; they never venture very far away from their homes, and the protection of their neighbours. Now and then a few Turkish women may be seen in the fields at harvest time, but even with them it is not a general practice. In Bosnia that is now all changed, and the women may be seen working in the fields every-

UNMARRIED TURKISH GIRL FROM MOSTAR.

where, as they do in Slavonia. Formerly, too, the rayahs built their houses some distance away from the high road, behind a clump of trees, or in a dip in the ground. Their own agha, or landlord, knew where they lived, but the sight of their houses did not excite the cupidity of any strange Turk who might happen to be travelling that way. Now that security is assured, houses are springing up in all directions.

ORTHODOX SERB.

A painful question was raised at the time of the insurrection which Mr. Evans has thus dealt with in a note to his "Illyrian Letters." "I must," he says, "while adding my homage to the painstaking character of Mr. Freeman's report, protest very strongly against some sweeping statements which he makes as to the morality of the Bosnian rayahs. After observing that the 'excesses and outrages' to quote our vice-consul's words, 'committed by the Bashi-bazouks last year, all over the country, were beyond description,' and mentioning that even respectable Turks had admitted to him that every possible horror had been perpetrated during the last two years,—Mr. Freeman further regrets to state that the Mahommedan landlords of this part of Bosnia, 'according to common report, have but little respect for the wives and daughters of their dependants,' but adds as a comment of his own, 'in a country, however, like Bosnia, where morality is at such a very low point, this last grievance, I should say, is not their greatest.'

"Now this statement as to the morality of the Bosnian rayah is cruelly untrue. Mr. Freeman has been doubtless misled by generalising from the state of the society in Serajevo, which is very different from that of the country districts. By travellers so well aquainted with Bosnia, as Ami Boué, Thœmmel and Roskievic, the peculiarly rigorous morality of the Bosnian rayahs, those at least, belonging to the Orthodox Church, has been made the subject of special eulogy. I will add that all I know myself of Bosnian country life, and all that I know from residents in the country, whose experience of Bosnia is far greater than my own, bears out the evidence as to the purity of their family life."

It happens that I am able to confirm what Mr. Evans says in the fullest possible way—not by the opinion of others, or of myself, but by the more convincing testimony of statistics. I have been furnished with the statistics of illegitimacy in Bosnia and the Hercegovina for the last ten years. Compared with those of any of the civilised countries of Europe they are so startling as to be almost incredible.

They are as follows:—

	Turks. Births.		Orthodox. Births.		Catholic. Births.	
	Legitimate.	Illegitimate.	Legitimate.	Illegitimate.	Legitimate.	Illegitimate.
1885	6,542	5	9,992	48	6,463	57
1886	14,854	7	23,452	88	12,273	96
1887	15,507	7	23,436	77	12,309	101
1888	15,030	14	22,083	96	11,212	112
1889	16,451	12	24,381	86	13,083	101
1890	16,042	9	24,427	106	12,641	98
1891	18,679	14	27,874	148	14,316	147
1892	19,358	15	26,705	136	14,001	171
1893	18,911	18	27,561	126	14,801	125
1894	19,223	10	28,597	163	14,443	176
1895	18,296	10	27,394	196	14,451	178

I felt considerable difficulty in believing that these figures could possibly be correct, but Colonel Cvjetićanin assured me that I might accept them unhesitatingly; that after his long experience of the country it was his deliberate opinion that no people in the world are so moral as these poor peasants. The question is of interest outside Bosnia, for I have repeatedly heard the same accusation brought against the Armenian women, and so far as I am able to learn, upon an equally baseless foundation, and I notice that in the accounts of the recent massacre at Egin, it is stated that fifteen women threw themselves into the river to escape outrage. The same thing was repeatedly done both in Bosnia and in Bulgaria. These figures prove that no greater morality is to be found anywhere in Europe than among these oppressed rayahs. "Certainly virtue is like precious odours, more fragrant when they are incensed or crushed; for prosperity doth best discover vice, but adversity doth best discover virtue."

I may add that, when talking to people in Bosnia about their kinsfolk in Macedonia, they have always dwelt particularly upon this question of the liability of the women to ill treatment as the chief of the miseries which that unhappy country has to endure.

CHAPTER VII

THE HERCEGOVINA—THE DEFILES OF THE NARENTA—KONJICA—
JABLANICA—SKETCH OF THE HISTORY OF BOSNIA AND THE
HERCEGOVINA

As I wished to see something of Dalmatia as well as Bosnia, I decided to go by sea from Metković to Spalato and to find my way back to Bosnia across the Dinaric Alps by whatever route I should find to be the most convenient. I did not regret my decision, as the line from Serajevo to Mostar passes through exquisitely wild and beautiful scenery. After leaving Ilidže, the train, with the help of a toothed wheel crawls up the flank of the Bjelašnica until it reaches the station of Ivan, at a height of 3,000 feet. There it enters a lengthy tunnel, on the other side of which it descends by a series of magnificent curves to the valley of the Narenta at Konjica, a town famous in Bosnian history for the persecuting edict enacted there against the Bogumiles. After that it follows the course of the Narenta to Jablanica through a pleasant valley enclosed by forest-clad hills. At Jablanica the character of the scenery changes entirely; the rugged peaks of the Prenj come into view, and the Narenta enters a series of extraordinary defiles, whose precipitous sides are often not more than a hundred yards apart. The river has fretted away its limestone banks from beneath, and evidently flows under vast overhanging eaves, for its channel

MOSTAR.

continually narrows down from a width of fifty yards to a ribbon-like stream of not more than seven or eight; in one or two places it is so contracted that it would be quite possible for a man to spring across. I have never seen a more picturesque river, or one so full of colour. The cliffs are of every shade of brown and purple and gray, and the sinuous thread of emerald flashing at their feet has all the look of a Turkish scimitar.

The Jablanica valley was the chief stronghold of the Bogumiles, who played so great a part in the history of Bosnia. It is difficult to acquire any definite idea of a country without knowing something of its past, so I will give a brief outline of it, derived chiefly from Professor Klaic's book on the subject.

Bosnia and the Hercegovina, though they are now and for several centuries have been, under the same government, were not always so, and geographically they are entirely distinct countries, quite as much so as Norway and Sweden, and with much the same kind of difference between them. Bosnia forms part of the watershed of the Black Sea, and is a land of sloping hills and fertile valleys. The Hercegovina belongs to the watershed of the Adriatic, and consists throughout of mountains of barren limestone, "Karst" as it is called, cleft by a succession of colossal ravines, with here and there an upland valley, or "Blato", which in winter and spring forms a lake, but in summer, owing to the drainage of the water through the fissures in the limestone, is converted into a luxuriant, though not very healthy, pasture. This natural division was recognized by the Romans, who drew a line from the present Banjaluka to the present Zvornik; all that lay to the north they included in the province of Pannonia, and all to the south in that of Dalmatia. It is a division adopted, too, by the people themselves. They only give the name of "Bosnia" to the district between

Serajevo and Zepće; that from Zepće to the Save being known to them as "The Posavina." The comparatively level nature of the ground rendered Bosnia easy of attack, whilst the narrow gorges of the Hercegovina, admirable for defence, made it a much easier matter to keep out invaders: so Hum,

KONJICA, HERCEGOVINA.

or Zahumlye, although feudatory to Bosnia, from the earliest times held better together, and as far back as the 10th century was an independent state under princes of its own. Its chief town in those days was not Mostar, but Blagaj, which was more than once destroyed, and is now a mere handful of houses. The Hranić, the princes of Hum, whose fortress of Stjepangrad dominated Blagaj, ruled as far as Almissa on the north, and as far as Cattaro, and even further, on the south. Their allegiance to the king of Bosnia was nominal, and in the year 1448 Stipan Vukčić declared himself independent, and assumed the title of Herceg, or Duke, whereby his country came to be known as "The Dukedom," the Hercegovina.

The original inhabitants of Bosnia were not the "Βεσσοι" a Thracian tribe, who, before they descended upon Bosnia, lived in Bulgaria, but an Illyrian race, which inhabited the whole of the western portion of the Balkan Peninsula, and whose only lineal descendants are the Skipetars, or Albanians.

Little is known of the Illyrians, and that little only of those that dwelt upon the coast, and had occasional intercourse with the Greeks, but it is thought that about 400 B.C. they were attacked by the Kelts or Gauls, who in a few years conquered the whole of what is now called Bosnia, driving the Illyrians into the present Hercegovina. There the latter held their own until the second century before the Christian Era, when they were assailed from the Adriatic by the Romans. Perceiving the greatness of their peril, the Illyrian tribes bound themselves together in a defensive league, the chief town of which bore the name of Delminium, whereby the whole of the confederated tribes acquired the designation of Delmatians, or Dalmatians. But their efforts were of no avail against the superior skill of their opponents, and in the year 78 B.C.

Dalmatia, and with it Bosnia and the Hercegovina, were finally subdued by the Romans, who combined the three countries into the Roman Province of Illyricum. Afterwards, when they had vanquished the Pannonians, and possessed themselves of all the land between the Save and the Danube, they gave the name of Illyria to the whole of the land lying between the Alps and Mount Dormitor, and between the Adriatic and the Danube. The name of Illyria as the name of a province then lost its original significance, and became a purely geographical expression, the different provinces comprised

MOSTAR.

in it being given the names of Dalmatia, Pannonia, and Noricum. Bosnia proved to be immensely rich in minerals, and the inhabitants, who until then had been wholly occupied with war and pasturage, were compelled to devote themselves to gold washing and mining, in which they rapidly acquired great proficiency. Gold is now found in Bosnia only in very small quantities. It has apparently all been worked out, for Pliny mentions that in the reign of Nero it was so plentiful that it was found almost on the surface of the ground, and as much as fifty libras a day could easily be collected.

The exact time when Christianity was introduced is not known, but it must have been at a very early date, for St. Paul in the Epistle to the Romans says that "from Jerusalem, and round about unto Illyricum, I have fully preached the gospel of Christ." Numerous converts were made, and in 303 A.D. they underwent a terrible persecution at the hands of the Emperor Diocletian, himself an Illyrian by birth, the ruins of whose palace still exist at Spalato.

ALBANIANS.

Upon the fall of the Western Empire in 476 A.D. Pannonia and Dalmatia came under the sway of the Ostrogoths, under whom they continued until 535, when the Emperor Justinian began a war with that people which lasted twenty years. During that time Dalmatia must have suffered fearfully both from war, and from religious persecution, for the ancient chroniclers mention that the heretical Arian Goths cruelly persecuted those of the true faith.

It was whilst this struggle between the Ostrogoths and the Byzantine Greeks was going on that the Slavs appeared upon the scene—first in the year 548, and again in 551. It is supposed that Theodoric, the King of the Goths, called them in to help him against Justinian. In 555 the Goths finally succumbed, and Dalmatia passed into Byzantine hands, but the influx of the Slavs was not thereby abated. They were joined by the Avars, who were also a Slav race. The most terrible invasion of the latter was in 598, when they laid waste the whole of Dalmatia. After that the Slavs, the "Βεσσοι," succeeded in making themselves masters of the entire country, and retained it until it was taken from them by the Turks in 1463, and they still form the bulk the population.

The Srbs and the Croats, or Hrvats, are descended from the same Slav stock, but the Croats were converted to Catholicism by missionaries from Rome, and the Srbs to the Orthodox Church by missionaries from Greece. This produced a lasting and bitter schism. The Srbi, or Serbs, have given their name to Serbia, just as the Croats have given their name to Croatia, but owing to some misconception Serbia has generally come to be known in Europe as "Servia," and the people as "Servians." As this is quite misleading I have adopted the names used by the Serbs themselves.

Bosnia under the Slavs was governed by her own princes, or Bans, until conquered by the King of Dioclea or Zeta (the present Montenegro) in 1082. From that time forth the unhappy country has known no respite from invasion, or from religious persecution. At the end of the twelfth century the

Byzantine Empire had become so weak that the Serb Tzar Dushan dreamed of founding a great Slav Empire, with Constantinople as its capital; and in all likelihood he would have succeeded in his design had the southern Slavs not had a more powerful enemy than the Greeks to contend with in the Hungarians, who on account of the Bogumile heresy in Bosnia, had enlisted upon their side the assistance of the Roman Pontiffs, whose power at that time was enormous, and who were in fact the dictators of Europe.

The Ban Kulin was at that time on the throne—the greatest of all the Bosnian princes. He was influentially allied, his sister being married to Miroslav, the Prince of Zahumlye, and under his wise and able rule Bosnia prospered so greatly that even now when the harvest is unusually good the peasants liken it to the harvests in the days of Kulin. During his reign the sect of the Patarenes, or Bogumiles, obtained a footing in Bosnia, and a still firmer hold in the Hercegovina. They were the precursors of the Protestants—the Christian socialists of that age. They called themselves simply "Christians," or "Good Christians"; the name "Bogumil" meaning "God's People." The founders of the sect came originally from Asia Minor, where they had assimilated the Zoroastrian doctrine of the dual principles of Good and Evil, Ormuzd and Ahriman, which is still held by the Parsees, the descendants of the Persian fire-worshippers. Marriage they considered objectionable much in the same way that St. Paul did. It was permissible, but they believed that it detracted from the higher life. They had no priests, only elders; and no religious ceremonies, the only prayer they used being the Paternoster; and they forbade the taking of oaths. The Bosnians are often reproached for the feeble resistance they offered to the Turks, but it should be remembered that the religion of the Bogumiles, which most of them had adopted, was much more nearly akin to Islamism than to Catholicism; so much so that the greater part of the people willingly accepted it, that being the reason why the bulk of the Mahommedans in Bosnia are Slavs, whilst so few of them in Serbia are.

From Syria the Bogumiles came first into Bulgaria, their tenets being brought thence into Bosnia and the Hercegovina by a Bulgarian priest, Peter the Bogumil. From Ragusa they found their way to Genoa. where they were adopted by the Albigenses. An old church is still standing at Albenga, near Genoa, from which place the Albigenses took their name, which is in the pure Orthodox style, severely simple and undecorated. The Albigenses, like the Bogumiles, were so cruelly persecuted by the Catholics that they were in fact stamped out, and the only remaining trace of this strange and interesting sect is to be found in Switzerland amongst the Vaudois.

Kulin reigned from 1180 to 1204, and after his

death Bosnia was governed by a succession of powerful Bans, who allied themselves by marriage both with Hungary and with Serbia. In 1353 Stjepan Tvrtko assumed the title of king. He it was who assisted King Lazar at the fateful battle of Kossovo. After that battle, instead of uniting with the other Christian Princes against the Turks he turned his arms against Croatia and Dalmatia, which he overcame, and of which he caused himself to be proclaimed king. He was a very powerful monarch, and if he had joined with Serbia and Montenegro against the Turks how different the fate of Europe might have been. In 1398 the Sultan Bajazid defeated Sigismund of Hungary at Nicopolis, and overran Bosnia with a huge army. Stjepan Tvrtko had been succeeded by Stjepan Dabiza, whose reign (1391–1398) was one of incessant conflict not only with the Turks, but with the Hungarians. His successor Stjepan Ostoja (1398–1404) wished to place himself under the protection of Hungary, and was in consequence dethroned by the Bosnian magnates, and Stjepan Tvrtko II. made king in his stead. He reigned from 1404–1408 when he was defeated and taken prisoner by Sigismund, and Stjepan Ostoja again seized the throne, which he retained until 1418. Both he and Hrvoje, the Duke of the Hercegovina, solicited help from the Turks, and with their aid the Hungarians were driven out of Bosnia. In 1444 Stjepan Thomas Ostojić ascended the throne. The whole of his long reign (1444-1461) was a continuous struggle with his rebellious subjects, most of whom had become Bogumiles, and whom, acting under the influence of Hungary and Rome, he so alienated by his bitter persecutions that many of them fled from the country and joined the Turks. In 1461 he was killed by his own son, Stjepan Tomasević, under whom the persecution became even more bitter, until unable to endure it any longer the people at last called in the aid of the Turks, and he was defeated and killed by the Sultan Mahommed II. at Jajce in 1463. Bosnia then passed into the possession of the Turks, in whose hands it remained until 1878, when it was occupied by Austria under the provisions of the treaty of Berlin.

CHAPTER VIII

THE VALLEY OF THE RAMA — MOSTAR — METKOVIC — SEBENICO — CAVES UNDER MOUNT TROGLAV — FROM SINJ TO LIVNO BY THE VAGANJ PASS — POLITICAL ASPIRATIONS OF THE CROATS AND SERBS

As we approached Jablanica we passed the entrance of the valley of the Rama, a little stream that flows into the Narenta from the north. At one time it formed the division between the two provinces; Rex Ramæ being one of the titles of the Bosnian kings. It is a lovely valley, in which is to be found some of the most beautiful scenery in the country. A diligence runs through it to Prozor twice a week during the summer, and thence over the Maklin Pass to Bugojno. Later on in the summer I walked through the valley, and while resting at a hán on the way met a Catholic Kmet of rather a better class than the ordinary peasant. He had just come back from his annual training, for military service is now compulsory both for the Turks and for the Christians. During part of the time they have to serve in Vienna, or Buda-Pesth, or Gratz; the Turks having with them a mullah, and proper arrangements being made for the cooking of their food. In Vienna a mosque has just been built for their use. He told me that he liked Vienna very much, that it was a wonderful town, and that he greatly enjoyed the theatres and the music, but that he did not like being a soldier because he had to leave his mother.

Family ties in Bosnia are very close, owing to the system of the Zadruga, or association of families in

THE VALLEY OF THE RAMA.

a joint community, which prevails amongst nearly all the Slav peoples. The women are respected and well-treated, though they have to take their share of field-work with the men and in consequence soon lose their good looks and the freshness of youth. The proprietor of the hán had a pretty little wife, who seemed to manage the inn entirely, for when I turned to pay him for what I had had, he beckoned to her to settle my account. It was harvest time, and he and his men were hard at work treading out corn with horses in the primitive fashion. I had acquired a few words of Slavonic, and in most places found it easy enough to get on with the peasants, but in the towns no other language than German is required. Even the peasants pick up a smattering of that during their military service. Slavonic is a hard language for an Englishman to learn, because it has comparatively little affinity either with the Latin or with the Teutonic languages, and English appears to present an equal difficulty to the Slavs. The Croats say that when the Lord God made the different nations he forgot to give them tongues, and when they came and begged for them, he took a piece of meat and cut it into

THE KAMA VALLEY. HORSES TREADING OUT CORN.

slices, and gave one to each to serve as a tongue; but the Englishman came late, and there was no slice left, so the Lord God gathered up all the odds and ends and put them together, and gave them to him for a tongue, and that is why the English speak so indistinctly.

I did not remain long at Mostar, though it is an interesting town, for it was hot and oppressive, and the mosquitoes were troublesome and peculiarly venomous.

A Slav dramatic company had just arrived from Serajevo, and I went one evening to see a performance of a play written by Prince Nicholas of Montenegro called "The Empress of the Balkans." It was received with breathless interest, and, though I could only understand the drift of it I could not help being moved by the general enthusiasm. The curious thing was that though it deals with the struggle between the Montenegrins and the Turks, several of the latter were there, and seemed to enjoy it as much as any one.

THE OLD BRIDGE, MOSTAR.

The old bridge, from which the town derives its name, has many legends connected with it. Some antiquaries think that it is of Roman origin; others that it was built by the Turks in the fifteenth century. There is no doubt of its great age, but it is still in good preservation, and is likely to remain so, as a new bridge has been built for the carriage traffic, and only foot passengers are now allowed to cross it.

The train which leaves Mostar early in the morning to catch the steamer for Spalato at Metkovic, took us down in two and a half hours. Several steamship lines have boats running, and there is a regular service both to Spalato and to Gravosa. How different things were when Mr. Stillman did the same journey in 1875. This is the description he gives of it:

"Metkovich is a wretched little place, which might be a flourishing port if there were not a Turkish custom house a rifle shot above it on the Narenta, and a Turkish administration beyond. Below it the Narenta widens out into enormous marshes, and loses much of its character as a river; but when the projected dyking, deepening, and draining are accomplished, the marsh will be a fertile plain, and the Narenta navigable for considerable vessels up to Metkovich. It is navigable now for steamers, but there seems to be little trade. Here we made a bargain with an Araba to take us to Mostar (nine hours); and your readers who know what it is to be jolted in a farm cart over a road, rocky or paved with unassorted pebbles, without being able to get refreshment of any kind on the way, can imagine the pleasure we found in these hours, of which at least seven was passed in a country without the slightest picturesque interest, every village by the way, except one Turkish, being burnt or demolished, or both; scowling Bashi-bazouks along the way in the hungry temper of mid-ramazan, and we the only Christians in sight. Among these irregulars were boys of twelve and fourteen years of age, with tufek and pistols, and all the swagger of incipient brigands. We had a large tract of forest to pass through, here and there a little tract being under a semi-cultivation. The body of a dead Christian lay by the roadside, covered over with stones and boughs; and the engineer pointed out to us by the roadside a Mussulman, who kept a raki shop near by, who had a few weeks before deliberately butchered and decapitated before his eyes a Christian engaged in cultivating his maize field, not a word having passed between the murderer and his victim previous to the attack. The engineer made a complaint to the authorities, and the Mussulman was put in prison for three days!"

The steamer called at Brazza, a little town built in a sheltered lagoon to evade discovery by the Corsairs, whose fleets used to sweep the Adriatic, and at several other places, and did not reach Spalato till six o'clock. I had just time to have a glimpse of Diocletian's palace in the waning light. The town, indeed, is merely the ruins of the palace, inside which the people have nested like pigeons. Early the next morning we left for Sebenico, a delightful, quaint, old place, built on the side of a hill, with the little narrow streets, the love for which the Venetians brought with them from their native city. The Turks never succeeded in gaining this part of Dalmatia, but they used to make raids into it and often came inconveniently near, as is shown by the following entry in the Diary of Marino Sanudo:— "December 2nd, 1498. By order of the Governor of Bosnia, 250 Turkish horsemen, at five o'clock in the morning, came with trumpets and standards to the villa Stintichi, twenty-five miles from Sebenico, and carried off 150 persons and about 6,000 animals. The Count of Sebenico, Arsenio Diedo, was desirous to send a messenger to the Governor to complain of what had been done, but could not find any one who was willing to go, because a short time before an envoy had been cut to pieces who had been sent to the Governor of Narenta concerning certain incursions which had been made by the Turks into the territory of Sebenico, and to ask for the return of twelve persons who had been carried away."

From Sebenico it is an easy drive to the famous Falls of the Kerka. They are very fine, and I was fortunate in the time of my visit as, on account of

Sebenico, Dalmatia.

[To face p. 96.

the heavy rains that had lately fallen, there was an unusual amount of water in the river. At the foot of the falls is a mill where the pyrethrum which grows all over Dalmatia is ground into the insect powder with which we are so familiar. It does not seem to be much used in Dalmatia itself, for I have seldom been in a dirtier country. The people are wretchedly poor, and travelling in the interior is decidedly uncomfortable; and even the seaport towns are not too cleanly. A railway goes from Sebenico to Knin, and from Knin I found my way by diligence to Vrlika, where I paid a visit to the caves of the Dinara.

Scarcely any one whom I met had ever heard of them, but they are really remarkable caves, of the same character as the mammoth caves of Kentucky. There are two of them, both situated at the foot of Mount Troglav, and close to the village of Cetina, by the side of which rises the river Cetina, a good sized stream which flows for a considerable distance through the interior of the country, and enters the Adriatic at Almissa. The entrance of the cave I went into was a small hole like the den of a wild animal. We had to crouch down and slide through a narrow slippery incline at the end of which we found ourselves in a spacious vaulted chamber.

DALMATIAN COAST, NEAR RAGUSA.

I had with me six villagers with lighted torches, so we went through cave after cave, until at last we arrived at a lake upon which the torches cast a flickering light, sufficient however to enable us to perceive that the water extended for a great distance and was very deep. I regret that I had not a collapsible boat with me, so that I could have explored further. We could judge of the great extent of the lake by the long continuance of the echoes of our voices when we shouted, and the peasants told me that the other cavern went for more than twenty kilometres into the heart of the mountain, and that no one had ever been able to reach the end of it. Some of the chambers were very beautiful, the stalactites in one, which they called the church, having quite the appearance of church columns. A number of fossil bones have been picked up in the caves from time to time, and as I was scooping up the soft damp ground to see if I could find any, I unearthed a human thigh bone: the remains of some poor fugitive who had fled there for an asylum, and had met his end from wild beasts or from the cold. On our way back, as we were making a short cut to the village, we suddenly came upon the source of the Cetina. I have never seen anything resembling it anywhere. It lay beneath us, a circular pool not more than fifty yards in diameter, of a clear deep blue, like a sapphire set in a girdling rim of rock. The sides of the pool, of hard limestone, go sheer down

DALMATIA

without shelving, and the peasants told me that they had been unable to reach the bottom with a rope a thousand feet in length. It is a funnel-shaped spring of unfathomed depth, and of an indescribable stillness and clearness. The water does not gush out, but wells quietly over without any noise, and with scarcely any perceptible movement. I have not the least doubt that it has a connection with the underground lake we had just left; the level of that being higher, it forces the water up the funnel, and so maintains a constant overflow.

SOURCE OF THE CETINA.

It is in fact a natural syphon. From Vrlika I took the diligence on to Sinj, and then went by the Bosnian military post over the Vaganj Pass to Livno, a long drive of nearly fifty miles, the road for the greater part of the way passing over barren limestone ranges. From Livno I went on again with the post-cart to Bugojno, the terminus of the branch line that goes through Travnik to Serajevo. The road was only interesting because the projected railway to Spalato, which Herr v. Kallay announced recently in Parliament had been definitely decided upon, is to take nearly the same direction. It will be a great boon to both countries, but it must take some time to make, as the ground over which it will have to pass is in places somewhat difficult, and in winter little or no work can be done.

Mr. Arthur Evans' predictions of the changes that the Austrian occupation would bring about in Bosnia and the neighbouring countries have in most cases proved to be true. But there is one question upon which I venture to disagree with him. He thought that, both in Dalmatia and in Croatia, the Serbs of the Greek Church held the future of their country in their hands, and not the Catholic Croats, who seemed to him to have little beyond a negative policy to animate and unite them. But the Illyrian Letters were written nearly twenty years ago, and the occupation has wrought a great change. There is nothing vague or halting about the policy of the Croats now. They aim at building up a Catholic Croat kingdom which shall not be merged in the Austro-Hungarian empire, like the Croatia of to-day, but shall be federated with it just as Hungary is. Their dream is to unite Croatia, Slavonia and north-western Bosnia in one great state, which shall have northern Dalmatia as its sea-board. The Croats have always been loyal to the Austrians, but a bitter hatred exists between them and the Hungarians, and their present political subordination to Hungary is productive of intense irritation. If an enlarged Croatia were given administrative indepen-

FALLS OF THE KERKA.

[To face p. 100.

dence similar to that now enjoyed by Hungary, it would assuredly augment the strength of the Austrian empire. This aspiration of the Croats is moreover perfectly legitimate, for the Orthodox Serbs in all the countries I have mentioned are in a great minority. In Dalmatia they only constitute 10 per cent. of the population, and in Croatia the proportion is, I believe, even less. What they hope to bring about is an historical as well as a natural connection; north-western Bosnia in pre-Turkish times being always closely allied when not actually united with Croatia and northern Dalmatia.

It is inevitable that some day this connection must be again restored, for the prosperity alike of Croatia, of Slavonia and of Bosnia depends upon their union with Dalmatia, and the prosperity of the barren strip of coast land which constitutes Dalmatia depends equally upon its union with the fertile lands that lie behind it.

But though the tendency of north-western Bosnia is to Croatia and not to Serbia, it is no less clear that the tendency of its eastern and southern borders is towards Serbia; and when the moment arrives for a final settlement of the country Austria will be wise if she frankly recognises both these tendencies. The Tzar Alexander, in the memorandum which he communicated to the English Government on June 8th, 1877, made use of these significant words :—
" These Provinces being situated conterminously with Austria-Hungary, give the latter a right to the

preponderating voice in their organisation;" and he added, "If Austria-Hungary on her side demanded compensation either for the extension required by Russia, or as a security against the new arrangements above mentioned for the benefit of the Christian principalities in the Balkan Peninsula, Russia would not oppose her seeking such compensation in Bosnia, *and partly in the Hercegovina.*"

No one who has witnessed the intense feeling which religious rivalry excites all over Eastern Europe can fail to understand why Austria, however excellent and humane her government may be, can never become an acceptable ruler to a Serb population, from the mere fact that she is Catholic, and they are Orthodox. The Serbs in Bosnia have every reason to be grateful for the change that Austria has effected, but they cannot help fretting under what is to them an alien rule. They kiss the hand they are not able to cut, but they keep the fire of their patriotism alight not for Austria, but for those of their own blood and of their own faith. And it must always be so. Catholic Austria can no more command the loyalty of Orthodox Serbs than Orthodox Russia can of Catholic Poland. It would be wiser to gradually build up a barrier of friendly states between herself and her arch enemy Russia, than to remain under the necessity of defending an extended and doubtfully loyal frontier.

At the present moment Serbia dislikes and distrusts Austria more than she does Russia because

Austria presses upon her border, and because proximity and the restrictions placed by the Hungarian Government upon the exportation of swine has given rise to considerable jealousy and friction. But in Russia, Serbia has, in reality, a far more insidious foe, and one more dangerous to her national independence. Most of her statesmen perceive this, but it is difficult to convince the mass of the people that what seems a merely problematical danger, though it is by no means so, is more to be dreaded than that which is close at hand and more apparent. An alliance between Austria and Serbia is of equal importance to both, but to enable Serbia to render efficient service to Austria, she must be accorded substantial support. To obtain an adequate return Austria must in fact make her friendship worth the having. Serbia is weak, but she could easily be made strong by giving back to her the major part of the empire that belonged to her great Tzar Dushan. Let her have Stara Serbia, Southern Bosnia, and the Hercegovina, with Ragusa as a port on the Adriatic, and Salonica on the Mediterranean, and she would be quite capable of holding her own against Bulgaria, even if Bulgaria were to fall entirely under Russian influence; and Austria would have converted a weak and unfriendly neighbour into a powerful people with interests identical with her own. It would be a wiser policy than attempting to govern unwilling subjects, and to obtain the adhesion of a nation which must always be hostile so long as Austria is in possession of what she believes should rightfully be hers.

The Emperor Aurelian withdrew his troops from Dacia, and tacitly relinquished that great Province to the Goths and Vandals. "His manly judgment," says Gibbon, "convinced him of the solid advantages, and taught him to despise the seeming disgrace of thus contracting the frontiers of the monarchy." It is a lesson that might be studied with advantage by England as well as by Austria.

CHAPTER IX

ZENICA—DERVENT—PRJEDOR—NATIVE RACES—DISAPPEARANCE
OF TRADE BETWEEN ENGLAND AND BOSNIA

AT the beginning of August, almost immediately after my return from Dalmatia, Baron Kutschera suggested that I should accompany Captain v. Roth, of the 8th Dragoons, on an official tour through the north and west of Bosnia, and I gladly accepted an opportunity of seeing the country in so thorough a manner.

We left Serajevo by train for Prjedor, reaching Brod late the same evening. As far as Kotorsko the line follows the course of the Bosna—a beautiful stream, flowing through a succession of fertile valleys, but unfortunately so full of shallows, that it has been found impossible to render it navigable. We passed the large town of Zenica, where there is a Government paper factory and a prison, managed on the Pennsylvanian system. Not far off beds of coal have been found; but like all the Bosnian coal, it is lignite, or brown coal, which burns away so quickly that it is not of the same value as if it were geologically ripe. That which is found in the hills of the Majevica, between Brčka and Tuzla, is, however, of a better quality, and is used on the Bosnian railway and by most of the factories; but wood is so plentiful and cheap, that in most private houses it is used in preference.

A few miles beyond Zenica the contracted stream of the Bosna makes its way through a narrow

RACES AT EYDI OR. PROCESSION OF MINSTRELS WITH WINNING HORSE.

gorge in the thickly wooded hills, one side of which is crowned by the old Turkish citadel of Vranduk, the Hawk's nest, stormed and taken by Prince Eugene, "Der Edle Ritter," in 1697, when he made his famous inroad into Bosnia. After inflicting a crushing defeat upon the Turks at the battle of Zenta, he crossed the Save at Brod with only 10,000 men, and marched rapidly to Serajevo,

Vranduk, and the other fortified places on the way being unable to resist him. But finding Serajevo too strong to be captured by assault, he retired as rapidly as he had come, satisfied with the blow he had inflicted upon the military prestige of the Turks, and with the proof he had given of the inherent weakness of their organisation. At Kotorsko the line leaves the Bosna, which flows another twenty miles before it falls into the Save at Šamac. Shortly before reaching Brod we came to Dervent, the centre of a thriving agricultural district. The population is mainly Turkish, and some terrible butcheries were perpetrated here during the insurrection. At Brod we changed into the train for Agram, arriving at Sunja, in Slavonia, at sunrise.  There we changed again into the little Bosnian line, made by the Turks, which extends as far as Banjaluka, reaching Prjedor at eight o'clock. After breakfast in a clean and comfortable inn, we drove out with Herr v. Szirmay, the Bezirks-Vorsteher (who corresponds to an Indian Deputy-Commissioner), to a plain some distance outside the town, where a horse show was to be held. I should explain that the Government has taken immense pains to improve the breed of the horses and cattle, and to induce the peasants to take proper care of their stock. They have established studs in different parts of the country for horses and mules, and every year horse and cattle shows are held in the principal towns, and considerable sums are given away in prizes. They have also started races for Bosnian horses, which create a healthy feeling of emulation. The prize giving was a lengthy matter, so I walked over to the Government Poultry Farm, where a great variety of birds are kept, both of game birds and of domestic fowls, the eggs being supplied free to such of the peasants as care to have them. It is found that the great difficulty in rearing the chicks is to protect them from the kites, which carry off large numbers. As there are no game laws in Bosnia, the game birds have been nearly all destroyed. Wild duck and quail are about all that are to be had, and even they are not plentiful. There are very few song birds, either; one of the most striking things in the Bosnian forests being their almost absolute silence. Fowls and ducks and geese are fairly plentiful and cheap. In the out-of-the-way districts, removed from the towns, a fowl can be bought for sixpence, and a goose for a shilling. But the commonest bird of all is the turkey, which is so universal throughout Bosnia that the Austrians call it the occupation bird. It was undoubtedly introduced into Europe from America, but it is curious that the name it bears in almost all the European languages is one denoting an Eastern origin. I have endeavoured to trace how this has come about, and those who are interested in the subject will find it discussed in a note at the end of this chapter.

The races were not until the afternoon, so we drove back to Prjedor to dine. It contains nearly 6,000 inhabitants, most of whom are Turks, and has

FOOT-RACE, PRJEDOR.

a considerable trade in cattle and grain. The river on which it is situated, the Sana, is navigable for small craft, which come up to it from the Save, of which it is a tributary. At the hotel we met a neighbouring landlord, a Turkish Beg, who told me that even now the richer Turks wear nothing but English underclothing, which they import from

Trieste, and that they will buy none that does not bear an English trademark. Before the occupation English goods had virtually a monopoly in the Bosnian market, but since Bosnia has been incorporated into the Customs Union of Austria-Hungary, Austrian goods are no longer liable to duty, whilst that upon those of other countries is so heavy as to be practically prohibitive; one of the most enterprising of the Turkish merchants assuring me that owing to the duty he had found it quite impossible to import English goods any longer. And the consular returns fully confirm this. They show that England has lost an annual trade of more than £400,000, the importation of cloth and woollen goods and copper having entirely ceased.

JUMPING ON INFLATED GOATSKINS.

The races were interesting and characteristic. In olden times the course was not circular as it is now, but the riders started from a point below the hills, and raced for a couple of miles straight across the plain towards the town. They rode barebacked, and as they neared the winning-post they threw themselves off in order to lighten their horses, which raced in by themselves. But so many accidents occurred that it has been made obligatory that the horses shall be saddled and ridden to the end of the race. The jockeys have no idea of a close finish, but get wildly excited, and gallop as hard as they can without looking round to see if there is any necessity for it; and as they come down the straight they drop their reins, and flog with both

RACES AT PRJEDOR.

arms as the man in this photograph is doing. Directly the race is over the crowd surround the winning horse and walk it round the course to the sound of drums and fifes and cymbals; hired buffoons shouting and playing antics in front of the procession. There were also foot races, and a national game which caused much merriment. An inflated goatskin is placed upon the ground, a ring is formed, and any one who chooses may jump upon it, and is of course bounced off in all sorts of uncomfortable attitudes amidst the laughter of the onlookers; the man who bursts the skin winning the prize. Last year the jumping went on for three days without any one succeeding in doing so, but this year a Serb boy did it after the first half-hour. The races seemed immensely popular. There were, I should think, more than three thousand people on the ground; and they had come, not only from Prjedor, but from Banjaluka and Sanskimost, and from all the neighbouring towns. Most of the people had driven over, but one or two were on horseback with a child sitting behind. It was a strikingly picturesque scene. The grand stand was gaily decorated with flags, and the people themselves were clothed in much brighter colours than is usual in Europe. It was quite like India; not only in that, but in the shouting and excitement of the crowd.

We left Prjedor again by the six o'clock train, after an enjoyable day. It was strange to think that it is the same place which has this sinister mention in Vice-Consul Freeman's Report of March 17th, 1876: "About a week ago the master of the Orthodox school at Prjedor was killed, and his head was paraded about the streets of the town upon a pole to the sound of drums and other music."

The distance to Banjaluka is not great, but trains in Bosnia go leisurely, and we did not arrive there

VRANDUK.

till 10 o'clock, tired and glad to get to bed, the hotel, like almost all I have stayed at in Bosnia, even in the most remote places, being clean and comfortable.

NOTE.

In Johnson's Dictionary the turkey is said to be a large domestic fowl supposed to be brought from Turkey, but it is now known that it was in reality brought not from Turkey, but from America, where two species are met with—the meleagris gallo-pavo and the meleagris ocellata, the native names for which are guajolote and guanajo. Prescott mentions that when the Spaniards discovered Mexico they came upon immense flocks of turkeys, which they called "Pavo" from its resemblance to the peacock, the Mexican variety having brilliant iridescent eye-like spots in the tail. He says that some writers had asserted them to be of African or Asiatic origin, but that Buffon had effectually disposed of that fallacy, and that they were certainly brought into Europe by the Spaniards after the conquest of Mexico in 1518, but he does not suggest any reason for their having acquired the name of "turkey"; a name so common in the languages of Europe that it would seem at first sight to point conclusively to an Eastern origin. The Serbs and the Bosnians call it "türke" like ourselves, and in Germany also it is known as a "trut hahn," or "türkischer hahn." The Italians and French, however, call it, not a Turkish, but an Indian fowl, the Italian name being gallo d'India, and the French d'Inde, a turkey cock being called a coq d'Inde; and curiously enough both in Turkey and in Arabia, it is known as the Hindu fowl. How then did it come to be introduced into all these countries from the East when it really came from the West. I think the explanation is to be found in the name given to the bird in India; "peru" being neither Sanscrit nor Persian, but Portuguese; so that it was evidently introduced into the country by the Portuguese. What happened was probably this: when the Spaniards discovered Mexico they brought some of the birds back with them to Spain, where they increased rapidly, and were taken for food upon other voyages because they are larger than fowls, and give more food without taking up a great deal more room, an important matter in the small ships of that time. In this way they found their way to Bombay, and were brought thence to Italy by the Venetians, so that in Italy and in France (it was the time of the French wars in Italy) they became known as the birds from India. For the same reason they obtained a similar name in Turkey and in Arabia. But they were evidently introduced into England and Germany not direct from India or from Venice, but from Constantinople, between which city, even after the Turks had taken possession of it, and England, there was always a considerable amount of trade. So that in these countries it acquired the name not of the Indian but of the Turkish fowl or "Turkey." It is an instance of the rapidity with which anything which is really of use will spread over the world. The potato, for instance, and maize, and tobacco, were all introduced from America, and in an incredibly short time were common all over the East.

That the turkey must have spread with almost equal rapidity is proved by Shakespeare mentioning it, though he lived so short a time after the discovery of Mexico. He only speaks of it twice, but he does so in the casual way which shows that it had already become a common domestic fowl. In *Henry V.* Gower says of Pistol, "See, here he comes, swelling like a turkey-cock." And in *Twelfth Night* Fabian says, "Oh peace, contemplation makes a rare turkey-cock of him. How he jets under his advanced plumes."

It is odd that the Portuguese should have called it "peru" instead of "pavo" like the Spaniards. They may have got it from Peru, and not from Mexico, or they may have picked it up in Brazil, where it is called "Pavo de Peru," for their ships were often driven there by the trade winds when on the way to India.

CHAPTER X

BANJALUKA—TURKISH BATHS AT GORNJI-ŠEHER—VALLEY OF THE VERBANJE—KOTOR VAROŠ

BANJALUKA was once a more important town than it is now; and I noticed that all over Bosnia the opening of the railway seems to depress the trade of the towns through which it passes. It is not so in other countries; and the statistics show that Bosnia as a whole is increasing steadily in wealth, the exports each year being greater. Why then are the towns in a state of commercial depression? Probably I think, because the country is poor, and its wealth almost entirely agricultural. Before the railway was opened, the cattle and grain had to be brought to the towns for distribution, and most of it was consumed locally, comparatively little being exported Now the produce is either sent direct from the wayside stations, or from those in the larger towns, and there is no longer the same necessity for markets. The little local industries too, are unable to compete with the cheap Austrian and Hungarian goods with which the country has been flooded, and in consequence the trade of the towns has diminished.

Only by visiting places away from the railroad, and seeing how backward they still are, is it possible to understand that any country in Europe can have been in so medieval a condition. In some of the villages the peasants had never even seen matches. They still struck a light with flint and steel as their forefathers did.

Banjaluka is prettily situated on the Vrbas, not far from where the river leaves the hills. At the time of the Turkish invasion, it was a powerful stronghold, but not of much importance otherwise. Under the Turks it became a rich and thriving town, and in 1871 had a population of nearly twenty thousand people, sixteen thousand of whom were Turks. Some of the mosques (there are forty-five in the town) are very fine, and one especially, that of which this is a photograph, is famous for its beauty. I was told a Pathan dervish was living here; and I found that a curious connection exists between the north of India and Bosnia. Not many years ago an Afghan prince who had to flee from

BANJALUKA.

Cabul settled down near Tuzla, and from time to time devotees passed through the country on their way to the tomb of a certain saint, called Gul Baba, who died in Buda-Pesth when it was in Turkish hands, and whose memory is much revered by the particular sect of Mahommedans to whom the Pathans chiefly belong. When the Turks were driven out of Hungary in 1691, a special clause was inserted in the treaty of Karlowitz that this tomb should be kept up, and it is still in existence.

GORNJI-SEHER.

In the afternoon we drove out to Gornji-Šeher, a pretty village built upon both banks of the Vrbas. The name means upper town, and is another instance of the mingling of Slav and Turkish words common throughout Bosnia, "gornji" being the Slavonic for "above," and "shahr" the Persian for "town." The Bosnian Mahommedans as I have before explained do not talk Turkish, and most of them do not even understand it, but a certain number of Turkish words have been introduced by the Osmanli officials. I use the word "Slavonic" advisedly because it is applicable to all the peoples who inhabit Bosnia, and who have really only one language. The Austrians, in the hope of welding all these conflicting Slav elements into a united nation, have introduced the use of the word "Bosnian," to describe both the people of Bosnia and the language which they speak. The difficulty in the way of realising this hope lies in the bitter antagonism that exists between the Orthodox and the Catholic churches; an antagonism which caused the fall of Constantinople, and that seems likely to be equally calamitous to the future of the Balkan States. M. Chedomille Mijatovich, in his valuable and interesting history of Constantine, the last Emperor of the Greeks, tells us that when the Eastern and Western Churches separated, in A.D. 1053, they did not part with sorrowing hearts, but with mutual anger and great bitterness, Pope Gregory VII. in a letter written in 1073 to Ebouly De Rossi, declaring it to be far better for a country to remain under the rule of Islam than to be governed by Christians who refused to acknowledge the rights of the Catholic Church. An even stronger feeling of detestation was cherished by the Orthodox against the Catholics. "Their excitement and hatred (I quote again from M. Mijatovich) became so intense that, as Ducas says, 'Even if an angel from heaven had descended, and declared that he would save the city from the Turks, if only the people would unite with the Church of Rome, the Greeks would have refused.'"

This feeling of mutual hatred has remained unchanged through all the centuries that have elapsed, and fellowship in persecution has not modified it in the least. "A false people the Orthodox, worse than the Turks," a Dalmatian Croat said to me; "if they ever obtain power here, I shall emigrate to America"; and the Orthodox distrust of the Catholics is equally strong, wherever they are; whether in Hungary, in Dalmatia, or in Bosnia, they call themselves Serbs, and cling with all the ardour of a long-enslaved race, struggling for freedom, to the dream of a glorious and united Serbian kingdom, which shall stretch from Salonica to Zara, and in which the national Church shall be the Orthodox. They therefore draw their inspiration from Belgrade and Cettinje, and use in their books and newspapers and writings the Cyrillic alphabet employed in Serbia and Montenegro, which is almost the same as that used in Russia. The Croats, on the other hand, aspire to the creation of a kingdom which shall include Croatia, Slavonia, Dalmatia, and Bosnia, and they employ the Latin character, because they look to Agram, and not to Belgrade, as the centre of their political and literary activity and thought. The feeling between these two branches of the same race is so keen that there seems little hope of amalgamation. The Slav newspaper in Serajevo has to be printed in parallel columns in Cyrillic and Latin, and by an order of the Duke of Würtemberg, who was Governor of Bosnia before Baron Appel, the official Gazette is issued in double columns also, the words in the two columns being exactly identical, only being printed in the two characters.

It is the hot baths of Gornji-Šeher that have given to Banjaluka its name; the baths of Luke the Evangelist, the holy Physician. One of them is said to date from the 6th century, and near it are the remains of one which is even older. That in which we bathed is quite new, and belongs to a fine-looking old Turk, who told us that he had always had a spring in his grounds, but that last year, after an earthquake, the flow of water became greater and more constant, and with more enterprise than Mahommedans generally show, he built a bath over it. The water was not particularly hot —about 22° C.—just warm enough to be pleasant. We sat afterwards on a divan in the outer room, and smoked cigarettes and drank coffee with the proprietor. That is a Turk's idea of pleasure; he will smoke and drink coffee the whole day long. I heard of an old man whose daily allowance is two hundred cups of coffee, and one hundred cigarettes. The proprietor of the bath was much interested in India, as indeed were all the Turks whom I met in Bosnia. He asked me many questions about the people, and the condition and status of the Mahommedans; holding up his hands in horror when I told him of the barbarous tribes who worship the Great Snake. He was interested, too, in our cameras, and in what we told him of photography, but he showed no undignified curiosity or unseemly surprise; in all his gestures there was the indescribable, reposeful grace, common to all Turks, which has so great a charm. They never raise their voices, or gesticulate, like the more excitable Christians; but are mindful always of the Prophet's command, " Be moderate in thy pace, and lower thy voice; for the most ungrateful of all voices surely is the voice of the ass."

We returned to Banjaluka along the other side of the river, the road passing between a succession of Turkish houses, enclosed in spacious gardens, belonging to men who had evidently at one time possessed considerable wealth. But most of them were dilapidated and uncared for, with signs of poverty cropping out everywhere. But the Mahommedan never complains, and, above all things, never begs. Indeed, one of the most admirable features in his character is the composure with which he accepts misfortune. "If you have, eat," says the Afghan, "if you have not, die." In Bosnia and the Hercegovina they have been treated with the greatest possible consideration, not merely because the country is as yet only occupied and not annexed, but because the Austrians, for political reasons, have deemed it advisable to show them especial favour. There are six hundred thousand of them, and about the same number of Serbs, while the Croats who only amount to three hundred and fifty thousand, and who are Catholics, can be disregarded. The

Serbs naturally incline to their kinsmen in Serbia and Montenegro, and the Austrians rule by placing them in opposition to the Turks, much in the same way as we rule in India through the antagonism of Mussulman and Hindu. But in Serbia there are not many Catholics, and hardly any Mahommedan Slavs, the few Mahommedans there being almost all true Turks or Osmanlis, and much harder measure has been dealt out to them than to their co-religionists in Bosnia. But I am told that they too bear their reverse of fortune with the same proud and uncomplaining calm, showing themselves true followers of Islam in its spiritual meaning of resignation to the will of God. Wherever there are Mahommedans, the same spirit is sure to be found; it is ingrained in them: "Those who behave themselves patiently in adversity, and hardship, and in time of violence, these are they who are true, and these are they who fear God." There is something ennobling in a religion which can exert so powerful an influence; but the fatalistic belief which is the keynote of a Mahommedan's life, and which gives him his stoical composure, has in it the germ of his decay. Of what use is it to struggle or repine if he believes as his sacred book bids him believe that the fate of every man has been determined before ever he was born. To fear God and submit patiently to whatever he may decree, may be productive of a certain nobility of character, but it will not promote progress, or help the world along like the belief does that God helps those who help themselves. It is touchingly significant that one of the books which appeals most powerfully to Serb and Croat alike should be Smiles' "Self-Help." A Croat told me it is more widely read in Croatia than any other book, and that he himself made a practice of always reading two pages of it every day.

We saw a good many children playing about in the road. I noticed that the hair of many of them was dyed red, and that many of the men dye their beards and moustaches red, or a reddish purple, just as they do in India. A beard is the distinguishing mark of a Mahommedan, for, by his religion, he is not allowed to shave. God intended him to have hair on his face, and it is wrong in him to remove it; a belief shared, as Mandeville mentions, by many of the orthodox Christians, "and also thei seye, that we synne dedly in schavinge oure Berdes, for the berd is token of a man, and zift of oure Lord." The children looked pinched and ill; with pallid complexions, caused partly I fancy, by the unhealthy, sedentary life they lead, for they never seem to have a good hearty romp, but in many cases also, I am afraid, from an insufficiency of food. The fare of the Bosnian peasant and of the poorer Turk, is always meagre. They scarcely ever touch meat, their usual meal consisting of a lump of black bread made from maize, Turkish coffee and a cigarette. With that he is quite content, but it is not nourishing food, and when in times of scarcity, it has to be reduced in quantity, he soon runs down in strength.

The rayah is generally tall and strongly built, but as a rule, he has little stamina, and is not capable of standing much fatigue. Centuries of oppression have dulled his faculties also, and he does not make nearly so good a soldier as the keen bright little Hungarian. But those who live in the hills are a much finer race than those who live in the plains and low-lying valleys, where it is feverish and unhealthy: and many of the Hercegovinians are particularly fine looking men. A good deal of stress has been laid by travellers upon the large stature of the Bosnian, but I think it is an illusion due in great measure to the loose garments he wears, and to his turban, which always makes men seem larger than they really are. The Afghans look exceedingly tall,

SELLING BREAD IN THE ČARČIJA.

but an Englishman dressed in their costume looks taller still.

In Consul Freeman's report, June 5th, 1877, there is this interesting passage in connection with Banjaluka. "I cannot refrain from mentioning one pleasing incident in connection with the flight of the Christian peasants from the neighbourhood of Banjaluka. On my late journey from that town to Gradishka, in the midst of the general desolation, I was surprised to see in one locality some houses standing and certain fields cultivated. On enquiry I found they all belonged to a rich Turkish proprietor, named Yusuf Bey Sibich. When the insurrection broke out and all the peasants were flying, and the Mussulman land-owners were seeking refuge in the towns, Yusuf Bey engaged twenty Albanians to guard his country house, and then calling around him his rayahs, he told them that if they wished they were at liberty to fly with the rest and he would not prevent them, but that he intended to defend his property to the last. If, on the contrary, they would stand by him, he would not desert them, and he trusted that this mutual protection and confidence would bring them all scathless through the difficulty. Yusuf Bey had always been a good and liberal master, and his peasants, without exception, determined to remain faithful to him, and up to the present moment not one, it is said, has either joined the insurgents or fled to Austria." The family of Yusuf Bey

Sibich, I am happy to say, still possess their father's lands, and hold an honourable position in the country.

Captain v. Roth had to preside at a horse show at Kotor Varoš, a place thirty miles from Banjaluka, and we drove out there and back the same day. The road passes between low wooded hills, for the greater part of the way following the course of the beautiful little Verbanje, an affluent of the Vrbas.

Kotor Varoš is the name of a district in which until lately there was no town at all, only scattered hamlets. It is one of the wildest and least culti- vated districts in Bosnia, and is noted for the number of bears to be found in the forests that cover the hillsides. Two years ago the government laid the nucleus of a town, which they have called Kotor Varoš, in the hope that it will bring the country-folk together, and open the district out a little. On our way we passed by the farm-houses of some of the Polish colonists who have done so much to improve the system of agriculture in the country. Their houses looked clean and neat, and the people well-to-do. They had, I was told, a hard struggle at first, though the government let them have the land on very easy terms, and they suffered terribly from the malarial fever which is the scourge of Bosnia, but they are hard-working and frugal, and now that they have got over the initial difficulties, they seem to be fairly prosperous and contented.

CHAPTER XI

JAJCE—FALLS OF THE PLIVA—SIMILARITY OF CUSTOMS BETWEEN THE MAHOMMEDANS AND THE CHRISTIANS—RELIGIOUS CONSTANCY OF THE RAYAHS

SERAJEVO, Jajce, and Banjaluka are the three oldest towns in Bosnia, and how little visited and how little known the country was in olden times, is shown by the fact that in both of the old maps I give later on, their position is wrongly marked; Banjaluka being placed to the south of Serajevo instead of to the north of it, and Jajce being placed where Banjaluka really stands.

The old road to Jajce goes by Varcar Vakuf, across the bleak mountain ranges of the Dobrinja Planina; but it is steep and difficult for carriage traffic, so the Austrians have made a magnificent new road along the valley of the Vrbas, which is a remarkable feat of engineering, the same level being maintained for more than fifty miles. The maximum rise is two per cent., and that only in one or two places; the road for the most part being absolutely even.

In all probability it will be used eventually for the

extension of the railway from Banjaluka to Jajce, the old road being quite sufficient for the limited traffic between the two towns. There is already a line from Serajevo to Jajce, and if it were carried on from there to Banjaluka it would put Serajevo in direct communication with Agram, and would be another step towards the completion of the greatly to be desired line to Salonica. The defiles through which the new road passes are very fine, but not nearly so grand as those of the Narenta, the hills being less lofty and wooded up to their summits, whereas in the Hercegovina they are bare and rugged. At the village of Bočac the government have built a comfortable little inn for travellers. They have also started a diligence, and seats can be had if there is room in the daily post cart. I mention these little details to show that travelling in Bosnia is not attended with either discomfort or difficulty. Where there is no railway or diligence, there is sure to be postal communication, and I have always found the post carts comfortable and remarkably cheap. So too is the railway travelling. The inns are generally clean and good, and the food very fair. I only remember two places where I was at all uncomfortable, and they were in districts far removed from the main lines of communication. I do not mean to say that it would be possible for a stranger to travel all over Bosnia without discomfort, for there are districts where there are no inns, only native háns, and where the government officials put up as we did in the gendarme posts; but there are comparatively few places where this is the case. As a rule travelling is as comfortable in every way as it is in Europe, and a great deal more so than it is in Dalmatia.

In the Jajce district the people have had so little intercourse with the outer world that they still retain their primitive costumes and manners. The men wear their hair long and unkempt, with hanging locks that reach almost to the shoulders. They invariably wear a red turban, and a rudely made sheepskin, in summer with the wool outside, and in winter with it inside. Their arms are generally profusely tattooed with religious emblems and devices. The women in their holiday dress are bedecked with silver coins and ornaments, and like the poorer classes in India, seem to wear the greater portion of their wealth upon their bodies. As we were nearing Jajce we passed by the church of St. John, venerated by Mussulmans and Christians alike, both believing that when it was threatened with destruction by the Turks the angels transported it bodily across from the other side of the river. Numbers of pilgrims of both religions resort to it on St. John's Day, in the hope of having their diseases cured. This is said to be due to a survival amongst these Slav Mahommedans of their ancient faith, which crops out here and there in other ways as a superstition. For instance, they will send for the Christian priest when dying, as well as for the

Mahommedan mullah; and several of the Christian festivals they observe as holidays. The 1st July, St. Elias' Day, is one of these, and so too is the 5th May, St. George's Day. On that day the Turkish maidens rise at four to wash their faces in the dew, in the belief that it will secure them a good complexion, and will keep them from becoming drowsy for the rest of the year. A similar survival is to be found in Bengal among the Hindus who were forcibly converted to Islam. I once came upon a curious instance of this in Calcutta. One of my servants, a Mahommedan, was taken suddenly ill, and a fellow servant, a Mahommedan also, came to me for medicine to give him. I poured some into a glass, and was about to add water to it from the caraffe upon my table, when he stopped me with—

"Sahib, not that water. He cannot drink it if you use that water."

"Why not?" I said. "He is not a Hindu. He has no caste."

"No, Sahib," he replied, "he is not, but he cannot drink that water."

There was no time to argue the matter, for the man was dangerously ill, so I told him to take the medicine away, and mix it with water himself; but the next day a mulvi happened to call, and I asked him if he would drink water from my water-bottle.

"Of course I would," he answered, "I would

drink water from your hand. We are not idolaters like the Hindus."

I thereupon sent for my servant, and the mulvi upbraided him for his ignorance of his religion; but when he had left the room he begged me not to be angry with him, because the poorer Mahommedans he explained, who live amongst the Hindus, have acquired many of their prejudices. It is more probable that there, as in Bosnia, it is the lingering influence of the original faith.

Jajce is one of the most singular towns in the world, with a picturesque beauty which is unique. The Vrbas, which here flows through a deep rift in the mountains, with lofty perpendicular cliffs on either side, is joined at right angles by the Pliva, which descends from the beautiful lakes of Jezero by a series of cascades extending one after the other for more than five miles, precipitating itself at last into the Vrbas over a cliff ninety feet in height.

On the right of the Pliva rises abruptly the conical hill upon which the town stands, and on its summit stand the ruins of the famous old fortress, around which are clustered the houses of the Turks, the Christian quarter being on the other side of the Vrbas; for the Turks guard with the greatest jealousy the privacy of their dwellings, and never allow those of the Christians to be near them. A more strangely beautiful scene cannot be imagined, or one more impossible to adequately portray, the charm of it depending in great measure upon the peculiarity of its colouring. The vivid green of the grass and trees, which are kept constantly moist by the spray from the fall, the blue and purple shades on the tops of the barren limestone hills, the picturesque Turkish houses clinging to the sides of the hill, and extending to the very edge of the cliff, and the brilliant rainbow which at certain times of the day shines through the mist rising from the seething caldron where the waters mingle, form a picture of unforgettable loveliness.

Jajce is the caressing diminutive of jaje, an egg, and various theories have been propounded to explain why the name was given to the town. Some antiquaries have suggested that it is due to the egg-shaped mountain upon which it is built; but the same word is often used to signify a jewel, and it is more probable that it received its name because it was looked upon as the jewel of Bosnia.

Apart from the beauty of the scene, my first feeling was one of surprise, if not of disappointment, to find the famous Jajce so small a place. It was hard to realize that upon this little town, scarcely bigger than a village, the anxious eyes of all Christendom were fixed, and that for many years it was the sole remaining barrier against the invading armies of the Turks. How it fell, and was retaken, and how long and gallantly it held out before it fell once more, have been told both by Mr. Evans and by Herr v. Asboth. Stjepan Tvrtko, the last King of Bosnia, fled there in 1462 before Mahommed II., but the persecuted Bosnians welcomed the Sultan rather than resisted him, and during his rapid advance more than seventy fortified towns, and finally Jajce itself, were surrendered to him without a blow. Stjepan was flayed alive by the conqueror, nor did their submission prevent many of the Bosnian nobles from sharing his fate. A few months afterwards Jajce, and the whole of northern Bosnia, were re-conquered by King Matthias of Hungary; and in the following year, 1463, the Sultan advanced

JAJCE.

against it with an army of 30,000 men, but after an heroic defence by Emerich Zapolya, he was obliged to raise the siege by the approach of King Matthias himself, and to effect a hasty retreat, sinking his cannon in the Vrbas as he retired. During the next fifty years both Mahommed II. and his successor Bajazid, made constant attacks upon the fortress, for, from its position, Jajce was, in a way, the key to central Europe; the Turks fearing to advance either through Hungary, or through the north of Dalmatia, so long as the Hungarians could endanger their flank from Jajce. The importance of the position, says Herr v. Asboth, "was so well realised on all hands, that the Pope appealed to all Christian Princes not to allow this fortress to fall.* Even Venice sacrificed money in its defence. In the year 1500, Sultan Bajazid led his army against Yaitze. John Corvinus, Matthias's heroic son, who governed that part of Hungary which lay on the further side of the Drau, defeated the Turks beneath the walls of the fortress, so that they perished by hundreds in the waters of the Verbas." Hungary herself was hopelessly crushed at Mohacs on August 6th, 1526, and two years later Jajce, and with it the whole of Northern Bosnia and Slavonia, and a great part of Croatia also, fell into the hands of Uzref Pasha, the Sandjak Beg or military governor of Bosnia.

Immediately below the fortress stands the ruined campanile of the church of St. Luke, graceful still in its decay. Herr V. Asboth mentions that Farlato, the Jesuit, states that, according to the tradition of the Bosnian monks, St. Luke lived and died in Jajce, and was buried in this church, but that when the Turks conquered the town, the monks managed to convey his sacred body secretly to Venice, where it now reposes. But M. Mijatovich, in his History of George Branković, has shown that this statement is erroneous, and that what really happened was this: St. Luke died in Syria, and his body was brought to Constantinople by the Byzantine Emperors, and when Constantinople was taken by the Normans in the thirteenth century, it was carried away to Rogus, on the Adriatic shore of Epirus.

In 1436 it was bought from the Turks by George Branković, the despot of Serbia, for the sum of 30,000 ducats. The Kaimakam of Rogus, fearing that there would be a dangerous riot if the Greek population knew that the town was to be deprived of the holy remains, secretly told the leading Greek families that he had received orders from the Sultan to make a census in order to impose a capitation tax, and that it would be well if they would leave the town for a few days, and go into the country, so that they might evade its imposition. While they were away he removed the body from the church, and delivered it to the representatives of George Branković, by whom it was interred with great pomp in Semendria, a town not far from Belgrade, and the then capital of Serbia. Branković was anxious to have it because an old man had appeared to him in a dream, and had told him that he must obtain the body of the evangelist and deposit it in Semendria, and the priests persuaded him that it was St. Luke himself whom he had seen. When his granddaughter Helen married Stjepan Tvrtko, the last King of Bosnia, she took the body with her, and placed it in this church at Jajce. She effected her escape when that town was taken by the Turks, and carried the body with her to Italy. Being in great straits for want of money, she was obliged to sell it to the Venetian Government, who placed it in St. Mark's. They tried to obtain it for a less sum than she asked by disputing its genuineness, and asserting that the real body of St. Luke was in a church in France; but she retorted that her grandfather, George Branković, was known to be a shrewd man, and it was not likely he would have parted with so large a sum as 30,000 ducats unless he had satisfied himself of the genuine character of what he was buying, and this argument seems to have convinced them. The whole story throws a vivid light on the curious superstitions of those times.

The rayahs in the Jajce district are almost exclusively Catholic. They are exceedingly bigoted, and ignorant, and some of their customs have a curious resemblance to those of the Mahommedans. Both the men and the women bring a prayer carpet with them to church, and when they kneel down upon it they slip off their shoes, and bow themselves down so that their foreheads touch the floor, just as the Mahommedans do. And like the Turks, the men shave their heads except for a little tuft of hair upon the crown. I noticed, also, an odd habit, which I have never seen elsewhere, and the origin of which I was not able to discover, that the men when they cross themselves before a shrine do not bend their knees, but merely lift up one leg. No doubt these peculiar customs originated in the necessity of conciliating their conquerors, in order to be permitted to observe their religion at all. The very name of rayah means "ransomed"—those who have merited death because of their unbelief, but who have purchased permission to live by paying a tribute. I do not think we western Christians, who have not undergone their fierce trial, appreciate fully the religious heroism these poor peasants have displayed during all the centuries they have been under the domination of the Turks. They have had to live in daily dread of martyrdom ; for the

CATHOLIC PEASANTS, JAJCE.

Mahommedans consider their lives to have been justly forfeited, and no Turk thinks he does wrong if he kills them. All this they have endured, though they have had ever before them the terrible temptation of being able at any moment to secure not only safety, but position and honour: for they have but to recant and embrace the religion of Islam to become not only free from danger, and insult and outrage, but to be placed at once on a level with their oppressors. One of the dying commands of the Prophet, a command which explains the rapidity with which the religion he founded spread, was that all proselytes should be admitted forthwith by the true believers to the fullest equality with themselves. Degraded and cringing as these peasants often are—and what race would not become so under similar treatment?—they have at least had the courage not to abjure their religion, and surely for this alone they have deserved the gratitude of Europe. Even with disaffection behind them the Turks proved themselves almost a match for western Christendom, and had they been able to advance, with these subject races not only not hostile but united to them by a religious enthusiasm, an enthusiasm which is always strongest amongst proselytes (as was proved by the ardour which animated the converted Bosnians and Albanians), it is hard to say where their arms might not have carried them.

CHAPTER XII

JEZERO – - VARCAR VAKUF—KLJUČ — THE BRAVSKA PLANINA —
PETROVAC—BIHAĆ—TURKISH TREATMENT OF ANIMALS

Our next halting place was on the Bravska Planina, a long way from Jajce, so we started at daybreak in an open carriage drawn by a couple of sturdy little Bosnian horses.

Although it was midsummer a thick mist shrouded the land until after seven o'clock, when it was dispersed by the rising sun. We regretted this the more because the scenery along the Pliva is said to be exceedingly fine, and Jezero itself is famous all over Bosnia for its beauty. Unfortunately we saw nothing of it, for, owing to the mist, we could not see more than a yard or two in front of us. The presence of so much water makes Jajce picturesque, but it also makes it feverish and unhealthy. At Jezero the Government have built a pretty little rest house, with boats and canoes for visitors who may wish to fish in the lake, which teems with trout. In the old days, a Turkish Beg who had a house there, used to take his women-folk out upon a couple of boats, lashed together in the middle, with a seat fixed athwartwise, upon which the ladies could sit without being inconvenienced by the waves raised by the sudden squalls to which the lake is subject. It was a Bosnian anticipation of the Calais-Douvres.

We refreshed ourselves with coffee prepared by a man, whose coffee-mill was a portion of the trunk of a tree, hollowed out at one end; he placed the coffee beans in the hollow, and beat them into powder with an iron pestle. He said it made better coffee and was more economical than the brass coffee-mills used in the towns, and that though it requires more time, in most of the country places the people prefer to use it. At Jezero we left the Pliva, and ascended to the crest of a mountain ridge, from which we dropped down rapidly to Varcar Vakuf, where we halted to dine and to rest the horses. It is a prosperous little town, the Vakuf kmets being the best off of all the kmets in Bosnia; why, I have already explained. The staple industry is carpet making, the carpets being handwoven, and having the harmonious colouring peculiar to the East. They are both cheap and good; one twelve feet long by four feet wide costs only £2, and is so strong that it will wear for years. Those I saw were free, moreover, from the aniline dyes which are ruining the carpets of central Asia and Kashmir. The town was full of peasants who had come in to make purchases, for it was market day. The principal articles for sale were the sheepskins, roughly tanned, and with the hair left on, from which the peasants make their "opankas" or shoes; knives of the distinctive Bosnian shape, women's aprons, carpets, and saddle-bags. Whilst I was making some purchases I ran up against a horse-dealer who had wished to sell me horses at Knin in Dalmatia. He told me with much satisfaction that he had done well not to let them go at a sacrifice, as he had obtained a good price for them afterwards in Bosnia. His servant was galloping a pony he was trying to sell up and down the hard road at full speed, rearing it up suddenly on its haunches with the powerful bit the Bosnians use. It was not improving for the animal, but it is the usual way in which the paces of a horse are tested by an intending purchaser. The bit is the ordinary eastern bit, and requires a very light hand; a bad rider will often cut a horse's tongue almost in half with it.

TURK SELLING COFFEE BY THE ROADSIDE.

Varcar Vakuf interested me especially from the contrast between what I saw and the state of affairs disclosed in Consul Holmes' report of 1873.

"Another vexatious affair has also just happened

at a place called Varsar, near Yaitza. The farmhouse of a Mussulman there was attacked by brigands, and his wife carried off and murdered, on which it appears from several letters which have been received here, that the local authorities seized, ill-treated and imprisoned all the Christian merchants of the place. The pasha says he cannot conceive it possible, and has made inquiries. The result will be, of course, that the authorities, and the medjliss of the place, will send a solemn declaration to the effect that nothing of the kind has happened; but at the same time, it is difficult to imagine that peaceable traders who have written to their friends here to say that they have been, and are still, suffering in prison, and begging them to take steps for their release, have entirely invented this story, however much they may have exaggerated it."

From Varcar Vakuf the road ascended gradually to the elevated plain of Rogelj, sheltered on all sides by mountains, at the entrance of which we passed by a simple memorial to the men and officers of the 53rd (Croat) regiment, who fell in the fiercely contested fight that took place there in 1878; by a curious coincidence, the day, the 10th August, being the anniversary of the battle. The campaign of 1878 was a short one, lasting barely three months, but the Austrians lost no less than five thousand men and a hundred-and-seventy officers. The hardest fighting took place in the district we were now going through. In one battle alone near Bihać, the Austrians lost eight hundred men. I do not know what the Bosnian loss was, but it must have been a great deal heavier.

The peasants hereabouts are poorer, it seemed to me, than in any other part of the country; and for miles of desolate moorland there is scarcely a

KLJUĆ—THE ANCIENT CLISSA.

dwelling to be found. At the extreme end of the plain stands a dirty little hán, near which is a curious Orthodox burial ground, the graves being marked by a long flat piece of wood with a diminutive cross piece at the top. Captain v. Roth, who knows every corner of Bosnia, said he did not think there was another like it anywhere. From this point the road wound down the mountain side to the valley of the Sana, the same river we had seen at Prjedor, which at Ključ flows through a narrow fissure in the hills, forming a military position of great natural strength, which has given to the town its name of Ključ, or key. The castle which overhangs it is now in ruins, but in pre-Turkish times it played a prominent part in the wars that were then so frequent. The road, an old Turkish road, followed the course of a ravine, and the descent was so rapid, and the turns so sharp, that in places it was almost dangerous. But the view was magnificent. Forests of primeval oak clothed the hills to their summits, and in the far distance we could discern the blue outline of the Bosnian Crnagora, or black mountain.

All the morning it had been oppressively hot, and soon after we left Ključ a heavy thunderstorm broke over us. The rain was tropical, and we were obliged to take refuge in a wayside hán, kept by a Turk, where we had the inevitable coffee and cigarettes. He told us he had bought the hán a year or two before, and that he had already recovered his outlay: a convincing proof of the increasing prosperity of the country. Night was approaching, and we had still a long way before us; so, in spite of the rain, we continued our way to the Bravska Planina, an elevated plateau, 5,000 feet in height, in the Dinaric Alps, the mountain range which separates Bosnia from Dalmatia. For the first six miles the road passed through a grand oak forest, which will be immensely valuable when there are greater facilities for transporting the timber. We then found ourselves on a wild bleak plain, stretching on either hand as far as the eye could reach, the bright green of the grass being flecked with white by the limestone boulders and ridges which crop up everywhere. There is no town between Ključ and Petrovac, a distance of forty miles ; so we put up for the night in the gendarme post which stands in the middle of the Planina. It was damp and chilly even then, and we were glad of a fire, and in the winter months the snow-drifts make travelling impossible, and the terrible north-west wind, the "bora" sweeps everything before it like a hurricane.

The following morning we continued our way to Petrovac, passing through immense herds of cattle, sheep, and goats. We were told there were as many as 80,000 head. But for the scarcity of water the Planina would be a magnificent grazing ground, but, as on all these limestone ranges, the water finds its way through fissures to underground caverns, and scarcely any is left upon the surface.

The herdsmen remain out all night with the flocks, merely wrapped up in their blankets. They looked wretched enough as they stood shivering in the mist which covered the ground in the early morning. There are no fences, and they keep their animals from straying by calling to them by name ;

for they are accustomed from birth to understand and obey the voice. They also have with them large dogs, very fierce, as they need to be, for they have continually to fight with the wolves, which in the winter become so emboldened by hunger, that it is by no means uncommon for them to tear a sheep out of the shepherd's hands. I noticed a curious habit among the Bosnian sheep which shows the frequency with which they are attacked. Instead of straying about singly upon the hill-sides, as our sheep do, they keep in little groups of from five to ten, grazing with their heads close to one another. I was told they do this instinctively as a kind of protection against the wolves. The dogs had to be held down as we passed to restrain them from flying at the carriage, and to meet them on foot is really an unpleasant adventure.

NEAR JABLANICA.

Petrovac, which with Kulen Vakuf is the chief place on this inhospitable plateau, is a miserable little town which suffered greatly from the want of water I have described, until last year the Government, with the anxious care for the development of the country, which I remarked everywhere, caused two reservoirs for rain-water to be built, one for washing purposes, the other for drinking. They have also erected a steam flour-mill, as there is no water available for an ordinary water-mill. The view here, though wild and desolate, is very striking. To the north and south extends an immense plain, covered with juniper bushes and oak scrub. Westwards rise the bare, rugged ranges of the Dinaric Alps; and on the east are the virgin forests of the Klekovača and the Crnagora, full of bears and wolves, deer and capercailzie.

The leading Mahommedan family in this district is that of the Kulenović, who claim a direct descent from the great Ban Kulen. It is pleasant to be able to recall Mr. Evans' account of the humane conduct of Ali Beg Kulenović at the time of the insurrection.

"Ali Beg Kulenovic, a fat jolly old Bosnian, who can drink his five bottles of rum a day, but is by no means a bad specimen of a Bosnian landlord, during the minor outrages of the first day's raid on the villages distinguished himself by saving some girls and women from the usual fate; well, if Omić's account be correct, he tried on the second day to exert his influence once more in favour of comparative moderation with the mingled gang of Redifs and Bashi-bazouks. But the Kaimakam, the representative of the Turkish Government, was for letting the ruffians have free vent. Words passed between the two, and as the Kaimakam was seconded by the more villainous among the Begs, he was able to seize fat Ali, who has since been languishing in a Turkish prison."

Ali Beg Kulenović is dead, but the Kulenović are still powerful landowners in Petrovac, and I had the pleasure later on, at the hot baths of Slatina, of being introduced to Mehmed Beg Kulenović, the present head of the family.

From Petrovac the road ascends to a still higher plain, many miles in extent, which terminates in a precipitous wedge-shaped hill, called the Ripački Klanac, from the summit of which we could see lying outspread before us the town of Bihać, and the beautiful valley of the Krain. Immediately below us was the deeply cleft ravine of the Unna, while upon the lower flank of the mountains on the Croatian frontier, we could see the grand old ruin of Sokolac, the Eagle's Eyrie, built by one of the Bosnian kings, of so massive a strength that its walls still remain almost untouched by time. The descent is appallingly rapid, and I held my breath several times as our Turkish driver, instead of keeping an eye on his horses, would point out to us the different places in the valley, driving, as he did so, unconcernedly along the very verge of the precipice. The horses had had two long days' work: the harness was flimsy, and held together with bits of string in the way familiar to those who have been in India, and if anything had given way, or if the horses had stumbled, nothing could have saved us from destruction; but the gallant little beasts trotted down as briskly as though they were on level ground. Accidents not unfrequently occur on these badly constructed Turkish roads, for though they are kept in excellent repair, it is not possible with so steep a gradient to obviate all risk of danger; and only last year an officer and his wife were killed in the Hercegovina, by their carriage capsizing and rolling over the precipice. How sheer the descent is may be judged from the fact that both of us felt an uncomfortable sensation in our ears when we reached the bottom of the Klanac, caused by the difference of atmospheric pressure between it and the top, and Captain v. Roth told me that he never came down it without experiencing the same sensation.

The distances the Bosnian horses will cover, and the fatigue they will endure, is really extraordinary. They are small animals, not more than fourteen hands in height, but full of courage, derived from the considerable strain in them of Arab blood. They are only watered once a day, and are fed on the coarsest and scantiest fodder; in consequence they look thin, but they are hard and wiry and capable of great endurance. These horses had brought us 110 miles in two days, during which time they had crossed three mountain ranges; and yet they trotted in the last ten miles as gaily as if they were at the beginning and not the end of their journey. The horse-shoes used in Bosnia, like those in use all over Turkey, are thin circular plates, with a small hole in the middle beneath the frog, in which stones are very apt to stick, the drivers carrying with them a hook-shaped instrument with which to extract them. They seem to suit the requirements of the country, for comparatively few of the horses go lame; and though they do not seem adapted to give the animals much grip with their feet, a Turk will ride recklessly down the steepest hill, and a Bosnian pony will clamber up a pathless, rocky hillside like a cat.

Not long ago there was a long-distance race from Bihać to Serajevo, the course being 170 miles in length, and passing over the mountains in the district of Travnik where the roads are one continuous up and down. The first horse did it in twenty-seven hours, dying within 100 yards from the winning-post; and several others came in under thirty-two hours. But we had a more striking instance later on of what the Bosnian horse is capable of in the ordinary routine of his life. We were on our way from Dervent to Šamac, and noticing that the horses were fagged and listless we inquired the cause of it from the driver, and he told us (he was only their driver and not their proprietor) that they had done a regular stage of forty miles a day for more than a month without a single day of rest; that, in fact, they had travelled 1200 miles in the month. The pack horses, when unloaded, are turned out to graze, or are tied up at the side of the road with a handful of grass to nibble at, with the pack-saddle left upon their backs. It is a clumsy cumbersome contrivance, which when once placed on a horse's back is seldom taken off again until it dies, though the poor beast is often terribly galled and can never enjoy a comfortable roll.

The Turks have the reputation of being kind to animals, and where kindness will cause them no personal inconvenience, I think they are. They are very neglectful; but are seldom wantonly cruel; that they would look upon as a sin. Bacon has an amusing comment on this trait in their character. "The inclination to goodness is imprinted deeply in the nature of man, insomuch that if it issue not towards men it will take unto other living creatures; as it is seen in the Turks, a cruel people, who, nevertheless, are kind to beasts, give alms to dogs and birds; inasmuch as Bus-

PACK HORSES.

bechius reporteth a Christian boy in Constantinople had like to have been stoned for gagging, in a waggishness, a long-billed fowl." I was told by a friend a quaint explanation given by a Turk of his objection to kill an ant: "I will kill a man," he said, "because he can defend himself, but I will not kill an ant, because it cannot." They believe, too, that every animal has a future existence; not with the vague belief of certain humane people amongst ourselves, but as one of the essential doctrines of their faith, a matter about which there can be no doubt, for it is explicitly stated to be so in the Koran, "the beasts which cover the earth, the birds which traverse the air, are creatures like unto yourselves. All are written in the book. They will appear again before Him."

As Mahomed's idea of future happiness was of a material Paradise, it was but natural that he should believe that all living creatures should attain to it; but I have been unable to ascertain whether they are to fulfil there the same functions that they do in this world. Will the sheep graze contentedly for ever, or will he be in perpetual oscillation between the shambles and the meadow? It is a curious problem which does not seem to have been thought out.

CHAPTER XIII

GRADUAL RELAXATION IN BOSNIA OF THE STRICTNESS OF MAHOMMEDANISM—DIFFICULTY FOR A MAHOMMEDAN TO SUCCEED IN BUSINESS—DEVICES FOR OBTAINING INTEREST—BIHAĆ—KRUPA—NOVI—TRAPPIST MONASTERY—HOT SPRINGS OF SLATINA—PRYNJAVOR—KARA-VLACHI—DERVENT

As we drove into Bihać we witnessed a sight full of prophetic meaning. On the outskirts of the town stands an Orthodox church, with a graveyard adjoining, and, close by it we met an old Turk driving a cart, laden with tombstones and Christian crosses. Our own driver, a Turk also, seemed as much impressed as we were. A few years ago such a thing would have been absolutely impossible. No Mahommedan would have so lowered himself. Now it is but one of many signs that the strictness of their religion is breaking down. Under the Turkish rule no swine were allowed to be kept. Now many of the Begs, although they will not keep them themselves, encourage their kmets to do so, and take the money resulting from their sale; and there is one wealthy Turk, who, I am told, does not scruple to keep them openly himself.

In like manner the Koran forbids the drinking of wine, but the emancipated Turk, not only in Bosnia, but wherever he is brought into contact with Western manners, finds an easy excuse wherewith to quiet his conscience. He will not drink *wine*, but he will drink beer, or brandy, or whiskey, or any other form of alcohol, because the Prophet only forbade the drinking of *wine*. These other drinks were not known when he was alive, and it was therefore not possible for him to forbid them. During a voyage from Port Said to Aden I shared a cabin with an Albanian, an officer in the Turkish army. We became friends at once; for, said he, "The Scotch and the Albanians are brothers. Are we not both mountaineers; and do we not both love whiskey?" It turned out that he had loved it only too well. He was seized one day, with a sudden and violent illness. I asked if I could do anything to help him, seeing that he was in great pain, "No," he said quite frankly, "I am afraid not. I am suffering from alcoholic indigestion. I have drunk a great deal in my life."

It is inevitable that the Bosnian Mahommedans must, under the new conditions, lose their proud position, and become mere herdsmen and hamals, or porters. They are seldom capable of business. Either they are exceedingly frugal and unenterprising, or if they break away from their tenets and traditions, they become dissolute and reckless, and squander their wealth in every kind of foolishness. Some of the Bosnian Turks, it is true, have tried to advance with the times, and one or two have amassed considerable wealth; but the majority have not progressed, and I do not believe they ever will. The principles of their religion preclude any hope of their being able to compete upon equal terms with other traders, and trade, in itself, is repugnant to them. In the Pathan villages, even those of the most fanatical tribes, a certain number of Hindu traders are always tolerated. They open up trade with other places, and save the Pathans the necessity of trafficking themselves, or of engaging in anything but agriculture and war.

I will take one instance only of the difficulties that lie in the way of a Mahommedan becoming a successful merchant. Usury is strictly forbidden, and a believer ought not, therefore, to put his money into a bank, or into any investment which will pay him interest. The injunction is clear; there is no escaping from it, "They who devour usury shall not arise from the dead, but as he ariseth whom Satan hath infected by a touch. This shall happen to them because they say, 'truly selling is but as usury.'" And wherever Mahommedanism is maintained in its integrity this precept is rigidly complied with. It is so, for instance, in Afghanistan, and all along our north western Indian frontier. A Pathan once consulted me how he should recover some money he had lent of which he could not obtain repayment. I advised him to bring a suit for it, with interest, which, as the money had been long due, would have amounted to nearly as much as the original debt. But he would not do this, "I am a Mahommedan," he said, "and cannot take interest. I only want my money back." And when he brought his suit, he did so only for the exact sum he had lent. In India proper, where for years they have mingled with the Hindus, and with Europeans, they have no such scruples; and in Bosnia, I found they have means, if they are so minded, of evading the strict letter of the law. They will not charge interest, but they contrive to obtain an exorbitant return for their money in other ways. A man will give another, say a sheep worth five guldens, on the condition that he is to receive an oka of butter, worth one gulden, every year till a sheep is returned to him; so that he is really getting twenty per cent. for his money. Or a man will lend a certain sum to another, who gives him a receipt for it accompanied by a promise to buy from him a gold watch, at an agreed price. When the money is repaid, the watch is paid for also, but is never delivered. Or there is a third way. It is forbidden to lend money at interest, but it is not forbidden to be a partner in a particular enterprise, and to share the profits that may accrue from it. This is frequently done.

Still, these are all awkward devices, utterly unsuited to the requirements of modern trade, and the bulk of a Turk's money, unless he puts it into land, is obliged to lie idle. Not long ago, one of the wealthiest of the Begs became insane, and when the Government took charge of his property, a great deal of money was found buried under the floor of his house, in the same way that treasure is kept lying unproductively in the Palace vaults of many an Indian Nawab. Under the pressure of Western competition all these restrictions are beginning now to break down. Many of the Bosnian Mahommedans will openly take interest, and have no hesitation in depositing their money in the Banks. I know one personally who has money invested in the Savings Bank at Serajevo. All this points to the likelihood of a gradual reconversion to Christianity. The taste for luxury has been acquired, the old simple ways and manners are dying out, and it is galling to a people who have once been dominant to feel themselves sinking step by step into the position of menials. They see that under the conditions of modern life, wealth alone can retain them in position and influence and power.

What, therefore, is more probable than that the younger generation should, one by one, abandon a religion which handicaps them so enormously. Mr. Evans' forecast of a general reconversion has not as yet come true; in great measure, I think, because the Austrians, with the hope of being able to support themselves by Mahommedan aid against the Slav population, which is to them such an unceasing perplexity and trouble, have treated the Mahommedans with greater consideration than the Christians, and so have preserved to them their feeling of pride, and to a certain extent, their sense of predominance. Mr. Evans, writing before the occupation, said " The nobles of Bosnia, whether Christian or Mahommedan, seem always to have valued their interests as a caste more highly than the creed they professed. Their tyranny has, on the whole, been more the tyranny of a caste than a creed. At the time of the Turkish conquest of Bosnia the forefathers of the present Begs renegaded for the most part, from a Puritan form of Christianity, and accepted the creed of their conquerors rather than sacrifice their possessions. There is indeed no prospect of such a severe alternative being placed before the Bosnian Begs at the present time, but there can be no doubt that even if it be for the sake of their social position, many of the Begs, if they must bow before the Giaour, will accept his creed. For them to-day, as at the moment of Turkish conquest, the chief anxiety is as to their position as a noblesse. Their rank secured, their future, political and religious, becomes quite a secondary consideration." Hitherto, the Austrian policy has been to keep the Turks apart from the rest of the people, and to prevent any such religious amalgamation, rather than to encourage it. So

CHANGE IN MAHOMMEDAN CUSTOMS

the Turks, being as they are, the most favoured portion of the community, have, at the present moment no active motive for change; but I have endeavoured to show that the change is nevertheless coming, not from pressure from without, but from far more permanent, though more gradual, influences from within. Before the occupation the manners of all the people, rich as well as poor, were frugal and simple, and the necessity for money was but little felt. But now that the Mahommedans have luxury all around them,

TURKISH HÁN, RAMA VALLEY.

and have, to a certain extent, indulged in it themselves, they will be unable to do without it; and in a contest between desire and principle, desire generally prevails if the contest be but sufficiently prolonged.

And there are many things that make it hard for a conscientious Mahommedan to succeed in business. His religious observances alone take up so much valuable time. Five times a day he must go to the mosque to pray. How is it possible for a man to compete with others in the face of such interruptions as that? Moreover, the whole teaching of the Koran is against the spirit of modern trade. So too is that of Christianity. But, as a rule, in commercial matters, Mahommedans conform to what their religion teaches them, while Christians frequently do not. Certain precepts of the Prophet have moulded the lives of his followers, and purified their everyday dealings. All over Bosnia a Mahommedan's word may be trusted in matters of buying and selling. He is bloodthirsty and treacherous, and cruel, but he will not lie, or cheat, or steal. Go into the Čarčija in Serajevo, and buy from a Christian or a Jew, and you must haggle with him, for you may be sure that he will ask you three or four times the proper price, but it is not necessary to do so when you are buying from a Turk for he will ask you only the real value of what he is selling. "Woe be unto those who give short measure or weight. Who when they receive by measure from other men take the full, but when they measure unto them, or weigh unto them, defraud. Let not these think they shall be raised again at the Great Day, the day whereon mankind shall stand before the Lord of all creatures. By no means."

We stayed at Bihać for two days, as it is an interesting town and the capital of Turkish Croatia, the Krain, or borderland, as it is generally called. It is one of the oldest towns in Bosnia and was built so long ago as 1214, by Bela IV., King of Hungary. Now it has a population of somewhat over five thousand people, half of whom are Mahommedans. That portion of the military frontier which lies immediately alongside it, has the name of "The Lika." It is a district which has furnished many notable generals to the Austrian armies, probably from the soldierly instinct acquired in many a border fray. Since 1878 many of the Likaners have settled in the Krain. We could distinguish them at once by their height, for they are all tall, and by their enormous mustachios, which they wear twisted upwards in a peculiar way.

Our next stay was at Novi, a town on the Slavonian frontier, forty miles from Bihać. The road passes through the little town of Krupa, which seemed in a very dead condition, with no trade or animation of any kind. The whole district, however, is wretchedly poor; scarcely anything will grow on the limestone, which crops up everywhere, and its wealth consisted entirely in its forests. These the goats

WOMAN SPINNING AS SHE WALKS.

have almost entirely destroyed, but, owing to the strict regulations enforced by the Government, the young trees are beginning to spring up, and before many years the country will be reforested. From Krupa to Novi we followed the course of the Unna, a lovely wild stream, descending, like the Pliva, in a succession of cascades. Those of the Unna are so small, not more than two feet in height, that they look like natural weirs, and many of them are utilised for mills, built on piles right out in the middle of the stream, and moored with heavy weights to protect them from the sudden floods, caused by the melting of the snow upon the hills. Among so rustic a people the miller is an important person. In Bosnia, as in Serbia, he is not paid in cash, but in kind; the usual arrangement being that he is to keep an oka of flour for every two hundred okas he grinds. There are many references to this custom in Serbian literature; it being a stock joke that the miller has taken more than his oka. Near Ottoka, —the island,—a charming little village half way between Krupa and Novi, we passed a pope or Orthodox priest in a carriage driven by a Turk, another sign of the change that is taking place. I noticed too, that the Turkish women here were not nearly so closely veiled as in the Petrovac district. Several whom we passed were working in the fields with no veils on at all. When they heard the carriage coming they merely ran a little way off, and sat down behind a hedge, or in a field of maize. Near Petrovac we encountered a woman riding astride, holding the reins in one hand, and an umbrella over her head with the other. She was not only closely veiled, but had a kind of mask over her face as well; but that was not a sufficient concealment, and as the carriage came up to her, she turned her horse off the road, and remained with her back to us until we had passed.

The Unna, like the Pliva, is strongly impregnated with lime, and the banks of both rivers are thickly encrusted with stalactitic deposits, which I was told make an excellent building stone. At Novi it is joined by the Sana, and a few miles further it flows into the Save. The country here being a broad valley with alluvial deposits is fertile and fairly prosperous, and Novi itself is a border town of some importance, as it is the terminus of a railway which was begun by the Turks for the purpose of connecting the Adriatic with the Mediterranean across the Sandjak of Novi Bazar. About sixty miles of rail were laid down from Novi to Banjaluka, and a similar distance from Salonica to Mitrovica in Macedonia, which is situated on the historic plain of Kossovo, the Field of Thrushes, in Stara Serbia. The line was intended to form part of the system of Turkish railways which was to have been carried out by Baron Hirsch, but which was never completed. Some day, it is to be hoped, the junction will be effected between Banjaluka and

Mitrovica; it would be by far the most direct route to India.

During the insurrection Novi and the whole of this part of the frontier were terribly treated by the Bashi-bazouks and by the Turkish troops. The villages were burnt, several rayahs were impaled, and other fearful atrocities were committed. Well may the poor peasants exclaim that where the voice of the Hodja is heard there is no peace in the land.

MAHOMMEDAN TOMB NEAR BANJALUKA.

From Novi we returned to Banjaluka by train, as we proposed to start from there for our drive through the Posavina, the borderland of the Save, the name by which the northeastern corner of Bosnia is known. Our first halting place was to be at Prynjavor, but we went a few miles out of our way to pay a visit to the Trappist Monastery on the Vrbas. The original monastery of La Trappe in Brittany was a Benedictine monastery, founded in 1140 under the auspices of St. Bernard. The monks had become very slothful and corrupt when they were reformed in 1650 by the Abbé de Rancé, who had renounced the world on account of the sudden death of a lady to whom he was about to be married. During the Revolution they were expelled from France and took refuge in Germany, from which they were also driven in 1868, and as none of the Christian states were willing to take them in, they asked and received permission from the Sultan to purchase land and build their monastery here.

Their life, in conformity with the rules of their order, is rigidly austere; full, not only of penitence and prayer, but of work. "Laborare est orare" is the keynote of their lives; and in truth the work they do seems to exercise a most potent influence.

It is difficult to understand how any human being can condemn himself to so hard a lot, but I was struck with the look of repose on most of the faces. The brother who escorted us round the monastery had been there seven years, and yet was a singularly cheerful, agreeable man.

As a rule the strictest silence is observed, speech being allowed only when there is absolute necessity for it, for the reception of strangers, the direction of workmen, or the transaction of business.

Not one hour of the day, from sunrise to sunset, is allowed to be unemployed either by work or by prayer. They have an orphanage, in which there are a hundred and seventy children; a spinning mill; and a sawmill, where they saw the timber for the different buildings they require.

Before leaving we were presented to the Prior,

who gave us a few kindly words of welcome. He told us his monastery had lately started a branch monastery in the Cape of Good Hope, some of the brothers going out from Bosnia to found it.

I asked him if the order had any monasteries in India or China.

"Alas! no;" he said, "the world is so full of shadows. There are many even here in Bosnia—it is not possible to deal with them all."

One may not accept the ideal the monks set before them—it is difficult to do so—but one cannot but admire the courage and constancy with which they carry it out, or fail to recognise the value of the work they are doing, by precept and example, in a semi-civilised country like Bosnia.

Their lives are indeed most hard and stern. Their fare is meagre; no meat, or butter, or milk. A pint of beer, a crust of bread, two or three apples, and an onion constitute their usual meal.

For exercise and recreation they walk in the graveyard, and when they die they are buried there in the garments in which they have lived, without coffins, and with no stone to mark their resting-place. And at night they lay themselves down on a straw mattress in the rough frock they have worn throughout the day.

Any one who desires to join them will be admitted, but he must first satisfy the Prior that he is not a fugitive from justice, and that he has no wife or children or parents dependent on him: if he has, he is told that his first duty is to them—a most wise and just rule.

The new comer has a probation of two years, during which time he may go back to the world if he so chooses, but at the end of the two years he must elect to go or to stay, and if he elects to stay he must remain until his death, on pain of excommunication.

It is strange that men should submit themselves voluntarily to so severe a discipline : but they believe they have their reward not only in the next world, but in this : in the composure which comes, they say, to almost all of them.

We saw the children playing happily in the courtyard. They looked bright and well, and it was evident the brothers do not extend their asceticism to them.

After leaving the monastery we drove through an exquisite beech wood to the hot springs of Slatina, which are much resorted to by the Turks. The water contains sulphur, magnesium, lithia, and a number of other ingredients, and has a heat of 50°C. Like the spring at Ilidže it is said to be very beneficial for rheumatism. When better roads have been made, and better bath-houses erected, Slatina ought to become an exceedingly valuable property, for the situation is lovely, but at present the baths are dirty and the accommodation bad.

On our way up the hill we disturbed an adder in pursuit of a frog. There are many of them in

Bosnia, and more still in the Hercegovina, but though they are venomous they rarely produce death. Last year a girl was bitten by one, and a gendarme who sucked the wound was attacked with paralysis and epileptic convulsions. He had to be discharged with a pension, and was taken into his own service by one of the Austrian archdukes. Since then, I am glad to say, he has quite recovered. The girl, oddly enough, suffered no bad effects whatever.

At Prynjavor we saw a number of the Karavlachi, a singular people who live in holes in the ground. There is a colony of them at Sitneš, near Prynjavor, which is the only place in Bosnia where they are found, their real home being in Transylvania.

They are not gypsies, though they lead the same nomad life, but are a distinct people with customs and manners of their own. The word "Karavlachi" means in Turkish "the black shepherds," vlachi being the same word as "wallach," which means a shepherd. The Turks used formerly to call all the Serb rayahs in Bosnia "vlachi," and the same name was given to them in Croatia, the Catholic peasants being called "Shokac" (Shokatz), because they make the sign of the cross not with the fingers, but with the whole hand.

Now, in the middle ages the northern part of Dalmatia was called "Morlachia." It bears that name in both of the old maps I have previously referred to, and around Knin and in the Lika, a considerable proportion of the population are still called Morlachs, and are of the Orthodox faith. Does not the name "Mor-vlachi," or "Morlachi," the black shepherds ("mor" being the Slav equivalent for the Turkish "kara"), point to the conclusion that the Morlachi were Serbs who retreated there before the advancing Turks and who dispossessed the Croats, by whom the land was previously occupied?

The Kara-vlachi wander all over Europe with performing bears, and Captain v. Roth told me he had seen one of them in London. They are not beautiful to look upon, and they are exceedingly dirty. I managed to photograph two of the women as they were walking along the road. They caught sight of me just as I was taking them, and were convulsed with laughter, as I found most of the peasants were when they were photographed. The idea is comparatively new to them, and they seem to find something very funny in it.

I was always careful not to photograph a Mahommedan unless he wished it himself: for the Koran forbids any representations to be made of the human form—lest it should lead to idolatry—and in many Mahommedan countries the people naturally resent being taken. But in Bosnia all such scruples are rapidly disappearing. I constantly photographed in

the open streets, and no one ever showed any sign of annoyance. Far from that, the people would come and look on: and a photographer told me that the Turks come to him to be photographed just as the Christians do.

From Prynjavor we drove to Dervent—a distance of twenty miles—through quite a different kind of country. We had left behind us the barren "Karst," the rugged, limestone ranges of western Bosnia, and had entered the fertile plain of the Posavina. The country is not unlike Sussex, rolling downs covered, not with forests, but with detached copses, and fields of luxuriant corn and maize. We noticed growing along the roadside great quantities of arnica, but I did not hear that any use is made of it.

At Dervent we were unable to get a carriage, and were obliged to go on to Samac in a country cart without springs. The peasants fill it with straw, and lie down and go to sleep in it. They put in for us what they called a "federsitz," a feather cushion as hard as a board, and excessively uncomfortable, and when we reached Šamac we were both of us bruised and stiff with the jolting.

THE CART IN WHICH WE TRAVELLED.

CHAPTER XIV

FERTILE PLAINS OF THE POSAVINA—ŠAMAC—GRADAČAC—ORAŠJE—THE TOBACCO PLANTATION AND GIRL LABOUR—BRČKA AND THE PRESERVED PLUM INDUSTRY—BJELINA—THE SALT SPRINGS OF TUZLA—LIGNITE SEAMS OF THE MAJEVICA—LIFE OF AUSTRIAN OFFICIALS COMPARED WITH THAT OF OFFICIALS IN INDIA

ABOUT half way from Dervent the road meets the Bosna, running alongside it until it falls into the Save at Šamac. It is a river that varies greatly at different seasons. In the summer it is sluggish, and full of shallows, but in the spring, when the snows melt on the mountains, the water comes down with terrific force, and rushes into the Save with such violence, that the current of that river is driven against the opposite bank, which it overflows.

Šamac is a prosperous, tidy little town with a considerable frontier trade. The Slavonian neatness and thrift has penetrated some way across the border, and the difference in cleanliness and order between the towns along the Save and the slatternly Turkish villages further inland is very noticeable. As at Brod, where there is a Bosna-Brod, and a Slavonian-Brod, so here there is a Šamac on both sides of the river ;

the two towns having much the same appearance, save for the minarets on the Bosnian side; for in the Posavina the houses are not made of wood, with thatched roofs, as in other parts of Bosnia, but are red-tiled, whitewashed buildings of the type found all along the military frontier. They are usually built on piles driven into the soft muddy soil. The dress of the women too is similar, but the men have not adopted the curious costume of the Slavonian peasants.

From Šamac we drove inland again to Gradačac, sixteen miles away. The land

SLAVONIAN PEASANTS.

is exceedingly fertile, as all alluvial plains are, and Gradačac itself is a prosperous little place, the Begs who have their estates there being amongst the wealthiest in Bosnia. Graf Rummerskirch, who kindly took us over the fortress, told us a story which reminded me strongly of India. There had been an epidemic of swine fever in Serbia, and precautions had been taken to prevent pigs being brought across the frontier, all along the road twig shelters being erected in which watchmen were placed to keep a strict look-out. Graf Rummerskirch asked one of the watchmen what he was doing, "Keeping a look-out," he replied. "For what?" asked the Graf. "I do not know," he said, an answer thoroughly typical of the Bosnian peasant. He is not stupid, on the contrary he is rather shrewd, but he will never give a direct answer if he can help it. Centuries of oppression have made him distrustful, and if questioned, fearing to be silent altogether, he takes refuge in "I do not know." The officers of the gendarmerie told me one of the greatest difficulties in collecting evidence in Bosnia is to get any answer from a peasant except this stock phrase. How like he is in this to the Hindu villager, who anxiously scans the face of his questioner to divine what answer he would like to have, and frames his reply accordingly; and if he has no clue to guide him, confines himself simply to "Khuda janta," God knows.

From Gradačac we went to Orašje, another village upon the Save. On the way we had an unpleasant experience of the changefulness of the weather. It had been oppressively hot all the morning and we thought a thunderstorm was coming. We had scarcely started when the rain began to fall in torrents, accompanied by a piercingly cold wind. We were in an open cart, and in a few minutes were soaked through and through, and chilled to the bone. We realised then the wisdom of what the country folks say, that when you go travelling you should always take your sheepskin with you, in winter you can wear it, in summer you can sit upon it and have it ready at hand, for you never know when you may be in need of it. It was so cold that when we stopped at a hán to get some coffee, the most stimulating and warming of all drinks, I was reduced to running up and down in the vain endeavour to get warm, and this was in midsummer, on August 18th, the Emperor's birthday. Whenever one travels in Austria it is impossible not to be struck by the strong personal influence of the Emperor over all his subjects. They are divided amongst themselves by powerful race antipathies, but they all display the same spirit

ŠAMAC.

of reverent affection for the Emperor. Even in Bosnia, which is only an occupied country, not yet incorporated into the Austrian Empire, this feeling was markedly apparent.

At Orašje the Wachtmeister at the gendarme post comforted us with some of the excellent slivović, for which this part of the Posavina is famous. It is made by allowing the plums to ferment, and

ŠAMAC.

squeezing the juice out with a press, and distilling it. What is made in this district has a peculiar flavour, because the stones, being crushed also, impart to the brandy the distinctive taste of the kernels.

Orašje lies low, right upon the river bank, and is therefore feverish and unhealthy; but the Government have lately constructed a dam, which keeps the water out, and in time the ground will become drier. All these riverside villages are subject to yearly inundations, which cause much damage and occasionally loss of life. But though the country is unhealthy the soil is marvellously rich, and there is little real poverty, the peasants being much better off than in the mountainous regions through which we had been lately travelling. We noticed, too, that the cattle looked particularly fine and well-fed. We came now, for the first time, upon the herds of swine which form the principal wealth of the neighbouring countries of Serbia and Slavonia, and which are kept here also, though in smaller numbers. One of these herds we saw swimming across a back-water, with the herd boy standing on the back of one of the pigs—a practical refutation of the popular fallacy that a pig cuts its throat when it swims. Sunflowers were in full bloom everywhere, lighting up the otherwise monotonous colouring of the landscape. In India they are thought to be, like the eucalyptus, preventives of malaria, and are often planted round tanks, in the hope that they will absorb the fever germs generated there. But both here and in Slavonia they are grown chiefly for the sake of the oil extracted from the seeds; most of the sunflower oil used in England coming, I am told, from this neighbourhood. One of the flowers was so enormous that we had the curiosity to measure it, and found it was just over twenty inches in diameter.

There had never been a horse show at Orasje

before, and the little town was gaily decorated. Many of the foals were excellent; much larger than those in Western Bosnia, the greater size being doubtless due to an infusion of Hungarian blood. After it was over a dinner was given by the Municipality, and the invitation to Captain v. Roth was kindly extended to myself. The speeches, which were mostly in Slavonic, were full of a natural eloquence, for all the Slav races seem born actors and orators. They have a true dramatic instinct, their words flowing easily and unconstrainedly, and their gestures being simple and unforced. But to me the most interesting feature of the dinner lay in the fact that the Burgermeister, a Mahommedan, formed one of the party, and was received on terms of perfect equality and friendship, not only by the Austrian officials, but by the Bosnian Christians, who were also present. It is strange that they should bear so little hatred to their former oppressors, and the explanation lies probably in the fact that they are all of the same race. Whatever the reason may be it fully bears out the contention of all who studied the country in Turkish times, that apart from the cruelties perpetrated or incited by Osmanli officials, and the habitual ill-treatment of the rayah women by the Beg landlords, which was in great measure a survival of feudal manners, the deplorable condition of the people was due to agrarian, rather than to religious causes, and that if these causes could be removed, the ill-feeling engendered by them would gradually die out.

In the afternoon we paid a visit to the Government tobacco plantation ; tobacco in Bosnia, as in Austria, being a state monopoly, from which a large revenue is derived. Permission must be obtained to grow it at all, and the grower may then only sell to the Government ; inspectors going round constantly to count the plants, and even the leaves upon each plant, to make sure there has been no infraction of the law. The tobacco grown in the Posavina is much ranker than that which grows further south and in the Hercegovina, and is only used for making the outside leaves of cigars. The leaves are tied up in bundles, and left to dry in sheds for a couple of months at a constant temperature of 60° C., which produces the slight fermentation necessary to fit them for consumption. The work is done by girls, whose hours are from six till six, during which time, however, they have three intervals for rest : half an hour for breakfast, half an hour in the afternoon, and two hours for the mid-day meal, which they bring with them ; so that, in reality, they have only a nine hours' day. For this they are paid eighty kreutzers, which comes to about ten shillings a week. So much has been written about the low wages, and the terrible sweating abroad, that I think it only fair to mention what I saw here. The rate of living is much less than in England ; but even if it were the same, the pay and the hours of work would compare favourably with those of the factory girls in the East End of London, the conditions of whose lives are in every way more trying than those of these girls. Wages, I found, varied, greatly in different parts of the country. In some districts of poverty-stricken Dalmatia, a man only earns twenty kreutzers for a day's work in the fields, but in most parts of Bosnia he can obtain from thirty to forty, and in well-to-do Slavonia from sixty to seventy, while these girls at Orašje get, as I have said, as much as eighty. Theirs is, of course, skilled labour, and they are only employed at certain times of the year, The work, moreover, is very injurious to the health, owing to the constant inhalement of nicotine —all factors that account for the high rate of wages.

From Orašje we went to Brčka, a commercial town twenty miles further down the river, with a population of six thousand people, about half of whom are Mahommedans. The banks of the stream are low, and on the Slavonian side afford no view of any kind; the vast plain, which stretches right away to Buda-Pesth, being almost on the same level as the water; but on the Bosnian side, the eye rests with infinite relief on the soft outlines of the distant hills. In its loneliness and silence it reminded me in many ways of the Hughli; with the same turbid, yellow stream, the same banks of crumbling loam, fringed with low-growing bushes, through which come glimpses of corn-fields and hedgeless meadows, on which herds of cattle are grazing ; whilst here and there a dense oak forest shuts out everything from the view except the interminable line of green against the sky. There is the same stillness and lack of traffic as on the Indian rivers : a monotony broken only by the picturesque mills built out into the stream,

BRČKA.

or by an occasional canoe, fashioned roughly from the trunk of a tree, and looking thoroughly Eastern, with its yellow sail and turbaned occupant. Brčka is built on slightly higher ground than Orašje, and is not therefore so subject to floods. During the palmy days of the Save Steamship Company it rapidly developed an important trade, and though that has fallen off a good deal since the steamers ceased to run, it is still a wealthy place, and must always be so, as the headquarters of the industry in preserved plums, which were formerly the staple, and indeed almost the only article exported from Bosnia. The heavy clay soil and moist climate, with its alternations of heat and cold, is peculiarly suited to the plum tree, and the fruit grown here is remarkable not only for the excellence of its flavour, but for the large amount of saccharine matter which it contains. Many of the "French" plums found on English dinner tables have, in reality, ripened here and not in France. The Government has been at considerable pains to encourage the trade, and the amount exported is increasing steadily every year.

From Brčka we drove through the hills of the Majevica-Planina to Tuzla, the centre of an extensive salt trade, as its name denotes, the word being derived from the Turkish word tuz, "salt." This part of the country before the Turks came was called "Soli," a word containing the Slav root "so," salt. In the Serajevo "Glasnik," Dr. Lljudevit Taloci shows that the name "Bosna," whether applied to river or land, signifies the place where salt is obtained, and it is noteworthy that the word "bos" in the northern Albanian dialect signifies salt-cellar, and also "saline" or place where salt is evaporated. Even in Roman times the salt springs were worked in a primitive fashion, and Tuzla has always been an important town, as it is the only place in the Balkans where salt is found. The Turks did nothing but work the surface springs, but, when the Austrians came, experimental borings were made, with the result that rock salt of a good quality has been found at a workable depth, and it is hoped that in time the whole district may produce salt in large quantities. After Serajevo

MILLS ON THE SAVE.

and Mostar, Tuzla is the largest town in the two provinces, containing close upon ten thousand inhabitants, the majority of whom are Turks, the remainder being mostly Orthodox Serbs. It has, therefore, been made the seat of a Vladikate, or Bishopric, under the control of the Orthodox Metropolitan at Serajevo; for one of the most beneficial reforms effected by Austria has been the substitution of a National Episcopate in place of the shamefully corrupt Phanariote Hierarchy, in whose hands the Turks left the control of the Orthodox Church and who were as great oppressors as the Turks themselves. The Phanariote Archbishop in Constantinople habitually gave the best appointments to Greek favourites of his own; and neither he nor they had any sympathy with the Slav rayahs who formed their flock; their one aim being to fleece them as much as possible. Now all these abuses have been abolished, and the priesthood has been purified and correspondingly strengthened. The present Vladika of Tuzla, M. Mandić, is, I may mention, an uncle of the well-known electrician, M. Nikola Tesla, who comes of a Serb family settled in the Lika.[1] A people who can produce such men as M. Marinovic, M. Ristic and M. Tesla, all of whom are of Bosnian-Serb extraction, cannot be said to be deficient in ability; they only require time to shake off the paralysing effect of centuries of ill-treatment.

As we were coming from Brčka, a Turk, who was driving the opposite way, pulled up by our carriage and told our driver in great agitation that he had left the passport for the cattle he was taking across the frontier (he was a cattle dealer) at a certain place in Tuzla, and begged him to go there and get it, and

[1] Since I left Bosnia M. Mandic has been appointed Metropolitan of Serajevo.

bring it with him to Brčka when he returned himself. "This," he said, holding up his right hand as he spoke, "I beg of you to do, in the name of God, and by the faith of the Turks, thou, who art also a believer." Our driver put up his hand also and said simply, "By our faith, I will do so," upon which the other went away perfectly satisfied, knowing that he would keep his word. The Serbs and Montenegrins swear in like manner by their faith, and all through the Balkans this oath by the faith seems to be the most binding a man can take.

At Tuzla there is now a lady doctor, holding a Government appointment; an excellent step in a forward direction, for a medical woman has opportunities to do good not only to the bodies but to the minds of the poor inmates of the harems, to whom the outer world is almost a sealed book.

In the Majevica-Planina we passed by valuable seams of lignite, which the Turks never made any attempt to utilise. These the Austrians began to work in 1884, and the opening of the railway to Doboj gave the enterprise an immediate impetus, and it is now in a thriving condition. There is also at Lukavac, eight miles from Tuzla, a sodia-ammonia factory which employs three hundred and eighty workmen. All these industries have been set on foot since the occupation, for the Turks never make any attempt to develop the natural resources of the countries under their sway. The main difficulty to be contended with at Tuzla is the scarcity of water; the Jalla, on which it is situated, being merely a brook, which in summer is almost dry. Consequently after the brine has been pumped up from the spring, it has to be run in pipes for three miles to Siminhan, where there is water sufficient to work the factory in which it is purified from the magnesia and other substances with which it is intermixed. From Tuzla we were able to go by train, as a branch line runs to Doboj, a station on the main line between Brod and Serajevo; the railway following the course of the Spreča, a beautiful little trout stream which flows through some lovely scenery.

After travelling all night we reached Serajevo once more after a three weeks' journey, during which we had visited the greater part of northern Bosnia and from which I came back with much the same feeling of admiration for the executive officers of the Austrian administration that is aroused by the labours of the same class of men in India. They lead for the most part a hard and lonely life of exile in uncongenial companionship; for to an Austrian service in Bosnia is almost as great an exile as India is to an Englishman. The climate, though not so bad as that of India, is far from healthy, and in the remote districts almost all whom I met complained of chronic ill-health. They have, too, the same separation from their children that the English in India have from theirs. There being, as yet, no suitable schools, for people in their position, to which the children can go, they are in most cases sent back to their parents' homes to be educated. The term of service before a pension can be earned is long, and leave is hard to obtain, the number of officials not being sufficient for the requirements of the country. Most of them are over-worked, and not too well paid for the services they render, although they are paid as much as the country in its present impoverished condition can afford. So like the Indian officials they work on from year to year, doing their work conscientiously and well, though they can form no permanent ties in the country. They live with the hope ever before them of being able some day to retire with a pension to their native land; for nearly all of them in Bosnia as in India, are aliens and sojourners in a strange land. They come to govern, but not to stay. In time, no doubt, the Bosnians will be able and will be allowed to take a larger share in the government than they now do, but at the present moment almost all the officials are Austrians. As a rule they are Poles, Croats, or Bohemians, or else they belong to one of the other Slav races included in the Austro-Hungarian empire, and who from the affinity which exists between the speech of all Slavonic peoples are more easily able to acquire the Bosnian language than the Hungarians or Austrians proper, to whom it is an unknown tongue. M. de Laveleye, writing in 1887, remarked that if Austria were to try to magyarise Bosnia she would end by being more hated than even the Turks. But so little has this been the case that, although Herr v. Kallay is himself a Hungarian, there are at the present moment only five Hungarian officials in the whole of the executive administration of the two Provinces.

CHAPTER XV

JOURNEY THROUGH THE HERCEGOVINA—DRIVE FROM MOSTAR TO RAGUSA—NEVESINJE—GACKO—INTERVIEW WITH BOGDAN SIMONIĆ—BILEK—TREBINJE—RAGUSA—CATTARO—SLAVONIA AND THE MILITARY FRONTIER.

SOON after our return Captain v. Roth was obliged to go to the Hercegovina, and asked me if I would again be his companion. The Hercegovina is a good deal hotter than Bosnia, and when we left Serajevo on the 27th August the heat was still very great. In the train I felt it even more than in India, as there were no thermantidotes in the carriages. On the evening of our arrival in Mostar there was one of the terrific thunderstorms which are so frequent in the Hercegovina. The troops who were bivouacking on the lofty Nevesinje plateau had an exceedingly uncomfortable three days, for the rain came down in torrents, accompanied by a piercingly cold wind. Gacko is ninety kilometres from Mostar, and we had a wretchedly wet and cold drive all day, and did not get in till late at night. A few miles outside Mostar, in the Narenta valley, there is a model vineyard, which the Government has started as a school for instruction. The wine made there is good, but very expensive, the ground being the hard limestone rock on which nothing will grow. It had to be broken up with dynamite, and mixed with soil brought from a distance before the vines could be planted. As an experiment it is interesting, but it would be impossible to cultivate in this way on a large scale, for the gardens could

BETWEEN TREBINJE AND RAGUSA.

never be made to pay. Then the road passes by Blagaj, and zig-zags up to the crest of the hills which form the left flank of the Mostar valley. We had on our right, on the precipitous rock out of which the river Buna flows, the ruined fortress of Stjepangrad, the stronghold of Stjepan Hvroje, the last Duke of the Hercegovina. All around us were rugged arid rocks, and as we looked down on the valley the only green spot we could see was the little oasis upon which Mostar has been built. The Hercegovina is a poor country, for though vines, tobacco, olives, and indeed fruit of almost every kind will grow luxuriantly wherever there is sufficient soil for them to take root in, the greater part of the land is, and must always be, an unproductive wilderness. The people, however, probably for that very reason, are both physically and mentally a finer race than the Bosnians, and they have that ardent love for their country which characterises all mountaineers. The Hercegovina is fortunate also in having a far smaller proportion of Turks than Bosnia. On the top of the hills we

MOSTAR.

found ourselves in quite a different kind of scenery, and for ten or fifteen miles we drove through undulating plateaux covered with dense forests, broken here and there by the stretches of the rich pasture land which constitutes the principal wealth of the Nevesinje district. Nevesinje itself is an ugly little town, only interesting because it was there that the insurrection began in 1875. The road then crosses a wide, level plain, at the far side of which it rises again to the ridge of the mountains, and

O

winds its way in and out between the peaks, at a height of 4,000 feet. During the winter months this portion of it is rendered impassable by the snow, and all communication between Gacko and Nevesinje is interrupted. Fortunately the road between Gacko and Trebinje is always open, unless the winter is unusually severe. The rain continued the whole of the following day, so we were able to see Gacko in its usual aspect. For the three summer months the weather is delightful, but during the rest of the year it is cold and wet.

Though the town looks small and insignificant, just a handful of houses huddled together on a bleak hillside, it has played a stirring part in Hercegovinian history, for being right upon the Montenegrin frontier it has been the scene of continual conflict, and has been burnt down and rebuilt time after time. The valley itself is fertile, but the greater part of it is still a swamp. The Government are draining this, and are building a dam across the mouth of the ravine through which the stream which feeds the swamp flows, so that the water can be controlled and made to flow into the proper irrigation channels. The work will cost £30,000 before it is finished, but the money will have been well laid out. It will all come back to the Government, before many years, in increase of revenue, and it will effect a great and permanent improvement in the country. As we were wandering about in the town we met a stately old man riding a spirited pony, whom Captain v. Roth told me was Bogdan Simonić, the voivode and popa, or priest of the Orthodox church, who played so prominent a part in the insurrection. He had under his command a large body of men, and his influence all along the frontier was great. He had a share in most of the fighting that took place, and himself defeated Djellal-eddin Pasha at Gacko with heavy loss. He is an old man now of over eighty, but he still performs his priestly duties, and looks as hale and hearty as a man of sixty. The Austrians have given him a pension, and a grant of land, and his three sons are all in good positions under the Government. The peasants still hold him in great regard; they have a saying the Gacko valley is very broad, and that the grey hawk (Bogdan Simonić) dwells in it. I was glad to have seen him, for he is one of the few still living of those who by their heroic revolt brought about the changed condition of this oppressed land.

HERCEGOVINIAN WOMEN.

From Gacko we drove along the Montenegrin frontier to Trebinje, passing through Bilek on the way. On all sides the country had the same desolate character. On the south rise the bare, treeless, waterless ranges of the Black Mountains, on the east and west stretches an arid plain covered with a scanty oak scrub, and fissured with deep ravines, which are not apparent until one reaches them; and on the north are the hills flanking the Narenta valley, over which we had just come. A mile or two from Bilek we came upon the source of the Trebinćica, one of those curious rivers of which there are so many in the Karst. Like the Buna and the Cetina it emerges in full stream from a cavern at the bottom of a hill, and after flowing fifteen or twenty miles disappears into the ground again a mile or two beyond Trebinje, only to appear once more as the Ombla, a river which issues from the foot of a cliff fifteen hundred feet in height and flows into the Adriatic, near Gravosa.

The road continues on the same high elevation until within a couple of miles from Trebinje, and the view, as the valley suddenly came into sight, was exceedingly beautiful. It was not until we saw how far below us the town lay that we were able to appreciate how great was the height at which we had been travelling since we left Nevesinje. The road, like all the roads built by the Austrians, is the perfection of a mountain road, the gradient never being steep enough to be dangerous or even inconvenient. Trebinje is a fine modern Italian-looking town. The old Turkish town was dirty and tumble-down, so the Austrians had it almost entirely pulled down, and a new one built in its place. From Trebinje we had only a short drive of twenty miles to Ragusa, the whole distance between that town and Mostar being 175 kilometres. The country never varies in character; all the way there is the same barren limestone plain, with a young oak forest springing up over it. We spent two very pleasant days at Ragusa, a charming old town, of which Mr. Evans has given a delightful account.

In its halcyon period it was almost equal in power to Venice, and was able to withstand the attacks not only of that Republic but of the Turks. It was here that Richard Cœur-de-Lion landed on his ill-fated voyage from the Holy Land. He had made a vow that he would build a church upon the first spot where he could effect a safe landing. He did so upon the island of La Croma, half a mile from the city, but the Ragusans treated him with such kindness that he petitioned the Pope to be allowed to modify his vow, and to build the church at Ragusa instead. As the Pope would not grant his request, he built a church in both places. That on the island is still standing, but the one in Ragusa was destroyed in the terrible earthquake in the seventeenth century, which gave a death blow to the already decaying fortunes of the city. But it still continued to be an independent Republic until it was acquired by Austria in 1797, with the rest of Dalmatia.

MONTENEGRIN.

From Ragusa we went by sea to Cattaro. The Adriatic coast is always the same. Lovely harmonies of colour between the cloudless blue of the skies, the deep blue of the water, and the changing grays and purples of the limestone hills. From the entrance of the Bocche di Cattaro to Cattaro itself is eleven miles, the channel in places passing through narrow openings in the hills, one of which is called the Chains of Cattaro, because in times of war a chain used to be stretched across it. Cattaro itself is not an interesting town, but behind it winds the wonderful serpentine road to Cettinje, the capital of Montenegro, the frontier of which begins at Njegusch, a little hamlet we could see high up on the hill above us. Cattaro is the natural port of Montenegro, and she has only been deprived of it because of her hereditary friendship with Russia, both England and Austria fearing that if she were allowed to have Cattaro it would be practically giving Russia a port upon the Adriatic. It is, I think, a mistaken policy; Montenegro is every year becoming of increasing importance, and in time is bound to obtain what is her natural outlet; to keep it from her is only making an enemy of her when she might have been a friend. For the same reason it is to be regretted that at the Congress of Berlin England should have demanded and obtained the suppression of the word "definitive" in the 2nd article of the treaty of San Stefano, that "The Sublime Porte definitively recognises the independence of the Principality of Montenegro" upon the ground that the English government had never recognised its independence.

We returned to Mostar from Gravosa by sea; a little coasting steamer taking us to Metković, calling on the way at Stagno, Trappano, and other seaport

THE SOURCE OF THE OMBLA.

towns, all having a strong resemblance to each other. The views everywhere are beautiful, but that at the entrance of the Narenta canal is singularly so, the river for some distance before it enters the Adriatic flowing through a broad marshy valley covered with rank vegetation, which makes it exceedingly malarious and unhealthy, but which affords a vivid contrast to the arid treeless hills which surround it.

I had spent a most enjoyable summer, and should have liked, before going away, to have seen something of the Drina and the Serbian frontier, and to have visited Vishegrad, and the Sandjak of Novi-Bazar ; but the weather showed signs of breaking, and travelling in the mountains was already uncomfortably chilly, so I accepted an invitation to go instead to Slavonia, as it was on my way home-

FORT AT ENTRANCE OF THE BOCCHE DI CATTARO.

wards. I had received many kindnesses in Bosnia, and bade farewell to my friends in Serajevo with a very real feeling of regret.

The train arrived at Vrpolje at the awkward hour of 4 A.M., but I found a carriage waiting to take me to Zupanje on the Save, some twenty miles away. The friends to whom I was going were English—the managers of a factory at Zupanje, for extracting tannin from oak wood, which belongs to an English company. The country through which we drove was a dead level; a vast swampy plain, periodically inundated by the Save. The roads are lined with poplars, as distinctive a feature of the Slavonian landscape as the cypress is of the Turkish; and in places we passed through the

CATTARO.

oak forests, which form the chief wealth of the country. The weather, fortunately, was warm and fine, though before I left I had a glimpse of Slavonian mud after a few days of rain. During my visit my friends very kindly drove me through the immense forests which grow along the side of the river. The Hungarian Government is systematically replanting the whole of the oak district. They have cut down the greater part of the existing forests, because an oak when it is more than two hundred years old deteriorates in value; it ought to be cut when not more than a hundred and fifty years old at the latest. When all the forests now standing have been cut there will be a gap of about thirty years, and after that there will be a regular succession of forests, so

STAGNO, DALMATIA.

that the industry will never be at a standstill; a very important matter for Slavonia, for the forests deliver altogether about 240,000 tons of cut and split wood annually, and 80,000 tons of tannin wood. The extraction of tannin is a comparatively new process. It was introduced into Slavonia by this English company fifteen years ago, but since then several other factories have come into existence. They are a fruitful source of income to the peasants, not only employing a large number of hands, but giving work to the villagers in carting wood, and in many other ways. Nothing is wasted in the forests. After the trees have been cut down the fragments are gathered up for the tannin factories, and any thing that is left is consumed by the charcoal burners. The total revenue produced is nearly a

ZUANE.

quarter of a million sterling (two and a half million guldens).

The strip of land along the Save, which extends about twenty miles inland, is known as the Slavonian military frontier. It formed part of the great line of the military frontier of Austria-Hungary, which stretched from the Lika in Croatia away down to the Transylvanian border. Now that Serbia is free, and Bosnia is in Austrian hands it is no longer needed, and has therefore been done away with, but it was of inestimable service in keeping watch and ward against the Turks at a time when they were still a formidable people. It originated in 1527, when the Archduke Ferdinand of Austria formed a corps of a thousand foot soldiers and two thousand horsemen to guard the frontier of the Krain. This was the beginning of what was afterwards known as the Croatian and Wendisch military frontier. Up to the middle of the sixteenth century it was under the orders of the General commanding in Gratz, and of the Captain-General in Laibach. In 1578 the number of the armed militia had increased to 6,780 soldiers, who were then put under special regulations and a special commander, and given corresponding privileges. As step by step the Turks were driven back from the lands they had conquered, so the military frontier was pushed further eastwards. In the old French map called the Dauphin's map and dated 1696, the tide-mark of their success is seen at its highest point. At that time they still held Buda-Pesth, which was included in the Beglerbeglicz of Bude, and the greater part of Hungary. But the very next year, in 1697, Prince Eugène won the battle of Zenta by which they lost the whole of Slavonia, and the frontier was extended as far as Syrmium. The Turkish reverses continued, until by the Peace of Passarowitz

[*To face p.* 204.

Part of a Map contained in the "Atlas Nouveau," by the SIEUR SANSON, published in Paris in 1696, and known as the "Dauphin's Atlas."

in 1718, Austria regained the whole of the Banat of Temesvar. A comparison of this map of 1696 with a map printed in London in 1726 shows how much ground the Turks lost in those thirty years. Since then they have been forced to retire from Serbia, from Moldavia and Wallachia,

SLAVONIAN PEASANT WOMEN.

from Greece and Bulgaria, and lastly from Bosnia and the Hercegovina. All that now remains to them in Europe is Albania, Macedonia, Rumelia, and Thracia, and they would long ago have been driven out of those Provinces also, had it not been for the jealousy between Austria and Russia, which the gradual destruction of Turkey has caused to spring up in the place of the old hostility to that Power.

It is lamentable to think that Hungary of all nations should be so ardent an advocate of the maintenance of the *status quo* in European Turkey, for had she herself remained under the power of the Sultan, she would never have been able to develop her resources in the marvellous way that has brought her so rapidly to the front. She would be in the abject condition of Macedonia and Rumelia, and she owes the fact that she is not in that condition in large measure to the efforts of that very Slav race whom she now desires to retain in servitude. The Croats, the Serbs, the Morlachs, and the Slavonians of the military frontier, all spent their lives and shed their blood in driving the Turks out of Hungary: for on them more than on any other of the races forming the Austro-Hungarian Empire, the burden of the conflict lay the heaviest —moreover it was not the original inhabitants of the Croatian and Slavonian borders who chiefly formed the frontier regiments, but fugitives from Serbia and the other subjugated Provinces. In 1690 no less than thirty thousand families fled from Stara Serbia into Hungary, under the leadership of their Patriarch Arsen Csernovics, and Leopold I., who was then King of Austria, in return for an asylum and for certain privileges claimed from them the duty of guarding that part of his kingdom which lay around the present town of Neusatz. The organisation of the frontier was peculiar, and worth recording now that it has become a thing of the past. There was no landed aristocracy; all the peasants being equal. They paid no rent, and scarcely any taxes, but instead were subject to the most exacting military discipline. Every family with three sons had to furnish a soldier; and if there were five sons two soldiers, who were maintained by the family, but received arms and uniform from the State. They remained on active service to twenty-three years of age; after which they were enrolled in the reserve. The

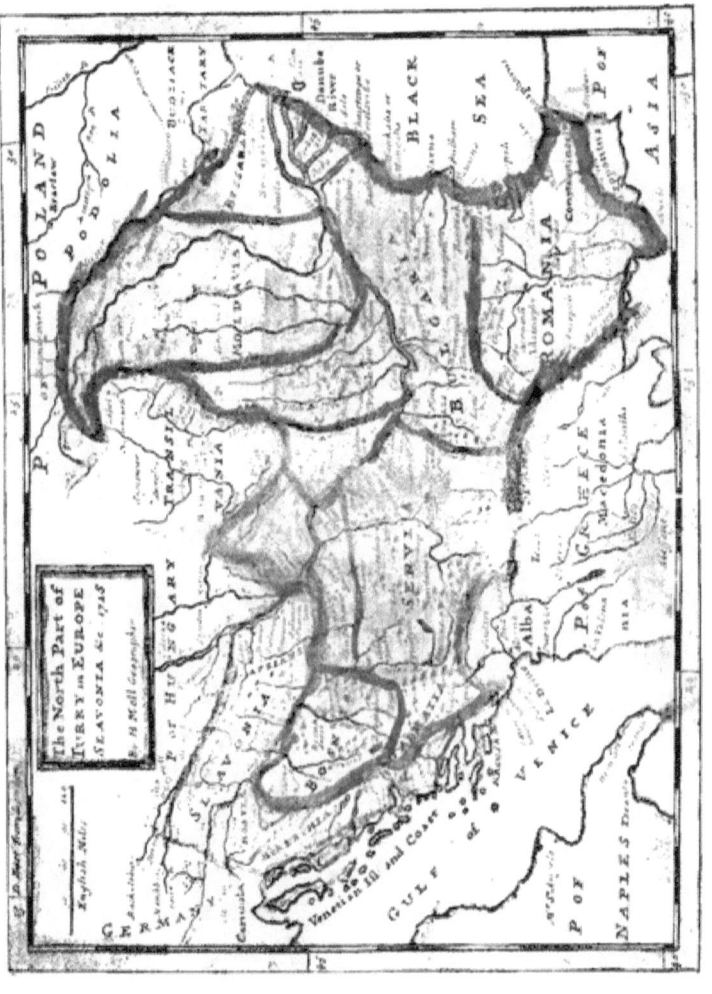

Map published in London in 1725.

[*To face p.* 206.

country was divided, not into districts, but into regiments, ruled by officers whose power was almost absolute.

In 1873 there being no longer any necessity for maintaining an organisation only fitted for troubled times, the regiments were disbanded, and the inhabitants of the frontiers were assimilated to the rest of the population of Hungary.

SLAVONIAN VILLAGE.

CHAPTER XVI

REVIEW OF ENGLISH POLICY IN THE BALKANS

I HOPE this brief description of a country still comparatively little known in England, may be of interest in itself, and I hope, too, that it may help to arouse a feeling of sympathy for the terrible state of Macedonia, the country which immediately adjoins it.

For it must be borne in mind that if Bosnia and the Hercegovina are now law-abiding, prosperous and comparatively free, only eighteen years ago their condition was as pitiable as that of Macedonia is now, and that the barrier which stood in the way of their deliverance, as it does to that of Macedonia now, was the traditional alliance of England with Turkey. Owing to our possession of India it is often urged that that alliance is an alliance of necessity: but it should be clearly understood to what it has committed us, and that England, more than any other of the European powers, is responsible for the desolation and misery of those portions of the Balkan Peninsula which have not yet shaken off the Turkish yoke. Lord Salisbury, speaking in 1877, said, "We feel that this is no common time in the history of England, and that we have laid upon us no common responsibilities by those who have honoured us with their trust. It is an anxiety which those who are connected with India feel specially because, rightly or wrongly, in the popular sentiment, circumstances have riveted the attention of the world upon what is supposed, directly or indirectly, to be connected with the destinies of India." And Mr. Bright, in a speech delivered about the same time, commented very forcibly upon what was undoubtedly, as Lord Salisbury said, the popular sentiment at the time. "Now that is the chief point upon which all this difficulty arises. England imagines that some great danger will happen to her; that she will lose her predominance in the Mediterranean, or that her route to India will be in some degree molested, if a Russian ship of war should come through these Straits, and therefore England is anxious to maintain Turkey in its present position, holding the keys of these Straits, and forbidding any portion of the Russian navy to pass from the Black Sea to the Mediterranean. Now you see, England—I speak now of England as it has been, and England as represented by the present Administration— England is afraid that if the Turk went out the Russian would come in, and therefore we are driven to this dreadful alternative, that we must support

P

the Turk with all his crime, and with all his cruelty, and we must support too, as we did practically support, the Mahommedan religion throughout the whole of that portion of the world. We give Bethlehem and Calvary and the Mount of Olives, through the blood and treasure of England, and the power over all these vast countries, which are almost a wilderness and a desert under the Turkish sceptre, —we do all this for the simple purpose of preventing Russia passing by any ships of war from the Black Sea to the Mediterranean."

Lord Hartington, too, during the debate on the Eastern Question in May 1876, used words which are worth recalling now—

"But let the House admit that a vast extension of British interests over the whole world may be a source of weakness rather than of strength. Our strength abroad, as at home, consists, I believe, rather in defence than in attack. In India, as elsewhere, I believe our true policy consists in consolidating our dominion, in guarding our frontier, and not in being drawn by every idle rumour, and every alarmist pamphlet from a position which is already strong. If it be necessary for the security of our Indian dominions that we should send forth armies to fight in Central Asia and in Asia Minor, I believe we shall find the task—I will not say too great for us—yet one that will tax our powers to the uttermost; but if for the security of our Indian Empire, it should be our fortune to contend against the forces of nature, or against the laws of human progress, then I say we shall have undertaken a task that will prove beyond our powers of accomplishment. There is no power which can restore the sap and vigour to the lifeless trunk, and there is no power which can check the growth of the living though struggling tree—the Turkish domination is the lifeless trunk, the struggling nationalities are the living tree—and this House is asked to-night to assert that with these nationalities, and not with the remnant of a shameful past, are the sympathies of the British nation."

The intimate connection and friendship of England and Turkey is no new thing. It is not a policy originated, as many persons seem to suppose, by Lord Beaconsfield. As far back as the 13th August, 1807, Mr. Canning wrote as follows to Sir A. Paget, who was at that time on a mission to Constantinople: "You will further state to the Turkish Plenipotentiary that in addition to this evidence His Majesty's Government have received the most positive information of secret Articles being annexed to the Treaty, from the tenor of which it is manifest that the dismemberment of the dominions of the Porte is not intended to be confined to the loss of Wallachia and Moldavia alone, but that it is in the contemplation both of Russia and of France to expel it from all the territories which it at present possesses in Europe. To projects such as these His Majesty's Government would never have been a party, and their only motive for directing you to communicate the existence of these designs to the Ottoman Ministers, is the anxiety to apprise them of the blow which is meditated against the Porte, in order that to avert it, they may exert all the means which they may have at their command. Whatever may be the ultimate success of these designs, His Majesty will always be disposed to acknowledge the Government of the Porte in whatever part of its dominions its residence may be established, and to maintain with it the closest friendship and connection."

But it is more especially since the Crimean War that England has been justly looked upon all through the Balkan States as the friend of the Turks and as the enemy of their Christian subjects. Dr. Sandwith stated what was but the truth when he wrote (in a letter to the *Daily News*) "of those dreaded English, whose terrible fleets have hovered off the coast, as in 1862, threatening the Christians if they dared to rise against the sublime Ottoman Porte; whose Consuls have always backed the authorities, sternly telling the plundered and outraged subjects of Turkey to 'look to their own Government for redress of grievances.'" How little the phases of the Eastern Question have changed in character. In August of last year Mr. Curzon, speaking in the House of Commons, said, "The Honourable Member (for Gloucester, had spoken of this island being surrounded by a powerless British fleet. That was not a correct description of the situation. The ships of the British fleet at the ports of this island had already rendered almost invaluable assistance, and more particularly at every port where ships had been stationed, the insurrection had been nipped in the bud when it was on the verge of breaking out." Sir H. Fowler thereupon protested against the absolutely neutral policy which the right honourable gentleman had propounded, which was not a neutral policy, but was one of direct sympathy with the Turkish authorities, tending to uphold a state of affairs which was a public crime, against which the better feeling of Europe had been openly expressed. They ought not to separate without saying that that was the feeling of the country."

And in yet another letter, written from Serbia to the *Daily News*, Dr. Sandwith (I make no apology for quoting him at considerable length, for no man had a more thorough knowledge of Turkey) wrote that, "after the bombardment of Belgrade by the Turks in 1862 (in the midst of profound peace), the Serbians made a desperate attempt to arm themselves. They were on the point of concluding a contract with a Birmingham firm when the English Government interfered and prevented the Serbians obtaining good English arms. They at last succeeded in obtaining some thousands of old Russian arms, which were conveyed across to Wallachia, when again our Consul-General (I had it from his own lips) did his utmost to stop them. All this time we were doing our best to arm Turkey. Read a speech of Mr. Layard's in the House of Commons in answer to Mr. Freeland's speech concerning Lord Hobart's report, and it will be seen that the Government of the day actually stooped to support Turkish credit in the teeth of that report and obtained for Turkey a fresh loan."

When, in 1876, the Bosnian struggle for freedom began, England again did all she could to discredit the insurgents and to assist the Porte. At the beginning of the insurrection Mr. Holmes, the Consul-General in Serajevo, wrote, "I am at present confined to my room with indisposition, but I intend to take an early opportunity of urging the Vali to take steps a once, if possible, to sweep these bands of brigands out of Bosnia." This was thoroughly in accord with the position taken up by the British Cabinet; Lord Derby, when agreeing to the appointment of a Consular mission to enquire into the state of affairs in Bosnia and the Hercegovina, doing so in these words, "Her Majesty's Government consented to this step with reluctance, as they doubted the expediency of the intervention of Foreign Consuls. Such an intervention, I remarked, was scarcely compatible with the independent authority of the Porte; it offered an inducement to insurrection as a means of appealing to foreign sympathy against Turkish rule, and it might not improbably open the way to further diplomatic interference in the internal affairs of the empire."

Moreover (I quote from the Duke of Argyll's book on the Eastern Question) " the British Government acted on an appeal from the Government of Turkey and directed our Minister at Vienna to represent to the Austrian Cabinet that Her Majesty's Government would be glad to learn that the Government of Austria-Hungary had taken steps to secure the peace of the frontier and to prevent the disturbances in Hercegovina from receiving support or encouragement from Austrian territory. On the same day similar instructions were sent to the British agent at Belgrade, through Sir H. Elliot, and that ambassador was desired, if he had opportunity, to dissuade the Prince of Montenegro from helping those who had struck for freedom."

When war finally broke out between Russia and Turkey the powerful Turcophil party strained every nerve to drag England into it on behalf of the Turks. Every effort was made to palliate the excesses of which the Turks had been guilty, and to represent the Russians as unrighteous aggressors.

Lord Beaconsfield, speaking at the Mansion House, said : " But although the policy of England is peace, there is no country so well prepared for war as our own. If she enters into conflict in a righteous cause—and I will not believe that England will go to war except for a righteous cause—if the contest is one which concerns her liberty, her independence, or her empire, her resources, I feel, are inexhaustible. She is not a country that, when she enters into a campaign, has to ask herself whether she can support a second or a third campaign. She enters into a campaign which she will not terminate till right is done."

And in a letter to the *Times*, dated the 4th January, 1877, Hobart Pasha made an appeal on behalf of the Turks which has a peculiar interest in connection with the recent massacres. "All the Turkish Government ask for," he said, "is this. It argues thus—We have never had a fair chance of doing right. Corruption, from the sovereign downwards, has been our ruin for many years. Now we are determined, under the auspices of our young, intelligent, and progressive sovereign, and such men as Midhat Pasha, to start on a right course. Give us a year to show what we can do (removing from our path foreign intrigue), and if at the end of the year we have not improved wipe us out of the map of nations, but if our fresh start is to be hampered by humiliations at the outset we can do nothing. Alas, I fear I know the answer too well, 'You have sinned too often to be believed'; but is such answer fair play, which is, as I have said, all I urge for my friends, the Turks."

The "young, intelligent, and progressive sovereign" to whom Hobart Pasha refers, is the present Sultan Abdul Hamid. And just as in 1877 Hobart Pasha pleaded that yet one more chance might be given to his friends, the Turks, so does Mr. Gibson Bowles plead for them now. "If the present destruction of Turkey," he said in a recent letter, "and of the Turkish Government, or of either, be sought, the task will be found impossible. But if the real reform of the evil Turkish system of government be desired, an opportunity is afforded now, and will probably remain open for the next few years, such as in all likelihood will never occur again. It is earnestly to be hoped, for the sake of Europe even more than for the sake of Turkey, that this opportunity may be taken."

Their attitude of hostility to the revolting populations the English Government never relaxed, either during the war or after it was over. The Duke of Argyll, speaking of the Berlin Congress, says: "The whole proceedings of the Congress have exhibited the English Government as jealous of, and hostile to, the growing power and advancing freedom of the Christian populations, and Russia as the only power which is heartily on their side."

Even after the Congress of Berlin, when a certain measure of freedom had been secured to them, the same spirit was unhappily maintained by England.

The Marquis of Bath, in his "Observations on Bulgarian Affairs," states that: "In all probability the English Consul-General has contributed in no small degree to the success of this, the most recent, and for the present the most prosperous attempt at self-government on the part of a province lately subject to Turkish rule. By his increasing hostility he has brought home to the Bulgarians the consciousness of there being among them an ever-present enemy ready to turn to account any mistake they may commit, and has impressed on them the necessity of sinking all minor differences in order to unite for the preservation of their newly acquired liberties."

"The Bulgarians," he says, "would willingly have looked to England, and courted her friendship in preference to that of any other power. England is distant; she has no frontier conterminous with her own; from her they know they need fear no aggression, nor any attempt at annexation. They would have welcomed English capital to develop their mineral and other resources, and would have been glad to find in English commerce a market for their produce. But the unvarying hostility displayed towards them by the English Government, the offensive tone of almost all its diplomatic agents, who have adopted and propagated every kind of report that could prejudice them before Europe, have convinced them that from England they can look for neither friendship nor protection; and they are at a loss to understand why they alone are refused the sympathy and support which England has invariably afforded to the cause of liberty in the case of other nations."

What a corroboration this passage is of Lord Derby's prophetic words spoken in 1864. "I think we are making for ourselves enemies of races which will very soon become in Eastern Europe dominant races; and I think we are keeping back countries by whose improvement, we, as the great traders of the world, should be the great gainers; and that we are doing this for no earthly advantage either present or prospective."

And yet this policy was spoken of by Sir Michael Hicks-Beach at Darlington on the 13th of last October in the following eulogistic terms. "The object of his (Sir William Harcourt's) detestation was the Cyprus Convention, and the traditional policy of this country in maintaining the Turkish Empire. That had been the traditional policy of our time. It was a just, wise and right policy, bearing in mind the dangers and difficulties that would arise on the dissolution of the Turkish Empire, so long as the Turkish Empire was what the Armenians would call a "live" Power, capable of reforming and improving the conditions of the populations living under it," and he concluded his speech with these words, "It was the proudest boast in the history of England that we had been fearless and active in promoting popular freedom and the welfare of humanity."

It is interesting to contrast this belief with Lord Salisbury's assertion in 1858 that "the consequence was that on the continent of Europe our claims to be regarded as the champions of liberty were looked upon as hypocritical boastings; for while we were loud in our professions we were lax in our practice."

That appears to be the opinion still of our conduct in Eastern Europe.

A recent Reuter's telegram from Canea, dated February 15th, states that "The British commander has threatened Prince George of Greece that, in the event of his executing the orders which he had received from the King and the Greek Government, he would be compelled to use force against him. This unlooked-for attitude of the British commander has produced a very painful impression upon the Cretan Christians, who regard the Prince as being sent to defend them from their Mahommedan foes."

Since then force has in fact been used, not against the Greeks, but against the insurgents. It is in every way regrettable that the bombardment should have occurred, and that the English ships should have taken part in it; for whatever the ultimate settlement of Crete may be, it will leave a bitter memory, both there and in Greece, which it will take years to eradicate; though it is becoming every day more apparent that it is due to the action of the English government that much harsher measures have not been adopted by the Powers.

CHAPTER XVII

A MAHOMMEDAN VIEW OF THE ARMENIAN MASSACRES, AND OF ENGLISH INTERVENTION—HOW THE SULTAN COMES TO BE CALIPH OF ISLAM—PRESENT CONDITION OF MACEDONIA

It may be objected that all the instances I have adduced date from some time back, but what I have myself seen this summer leads me to think that this feeling of distrust of England exists as strongly as ever; and having regard to our actions in the past, it is but natural that this should be so; and that it should be thought that our jealousy of Russia will always overpower every other feeling.

Moreover the Turks believe, that from our possession of India, we are bound to stand by them whatever they may do. I was talking with one of them in Serajevo about other matters, when he suddenly burst out with: "Why are you English making so much trouble about Armenia?" "Well," I answered, "what have you been doing there?" "They began it," he said; "they killed the Mahommedans in the Mosques." "Let us grant that they did; when Russia, or Austria, or England, have to deal with rebels they shoot them down or execute them, but they do not torture them, nor do they kill women and children, as you have been doing." He shrugged his shoulders, and repeated, "They began it, and it is not right that England, which is the greatest Mahommedan Power in the world, should arouse feeling in this way against the Sultan." "It is quite time," I answered, "that you should understand that the English are tired of this kind of thing, and that they are determined that come what will these massacres shall cease." "But," he insisted, "if you try to coerce the Sultan by forcible means, you will find that your Mahommedan soldiers in India will not be very well pleased." "There are many Englishmen," I said, "who would rather run the risk of losing India altogether than that England should be allied any longer with a man who has been guilty of such abominable deeds; but I do not think there would be any such danger as you suggest, for if you will think the matter over for a moment you will see that your argument is not a good one. You must remember that although we have a great many Mahommedans in India we have more than twice as many Hindus. Apart from that, however, I do not think the Indian Mahommedans look to Constantinople so much as they do to Mecca; and I do not believe that even our open hostility to the Sultan would affect them in the least." "I assure you," he said earnestly, "that you are quite wrong, and that every Mahommedan, wherever he is, every Friday when he goes to the Mosque, prays for the Sultan, as the Caliph of Islam."

Now I believe this assertion is not quite accurate. In Bosnia, it is true, the Mahommedans pray for the Sultan, because he is still the nominal sovereign of the country, but they also pray for the Emperor Francis Joseph. I am not aware of the custom among the Russian Mahommedans, but in India the prayer, the Khutbah, as it is called, runs thus, "O God, bless the King of the age, and make him kind and favourable to the people." In Algiers the Mahommedans are only allowed to pray for those of the true faith, and the protectors thereof. I am not sure of the exact form of words, but the prayer was carefully drawn up by the French at the time the country was acquired, so as to avoid any kind of acknowledgment of the Sultan's suzerainty.

The argument, however, has been constantly made use of by those who wish to draw closer the connection between England and Turkey.

It was stated very clearly in an article on Indian affairs, published in the *Times* on the 28th December last :—

"The coercion of the Sultan is being keenly watched, but with mixed feelings, in India. The Hindu Press regards it from the humanitarian point of view, which has consistently guided the action of the British Government. But to fifty millions of our Indian subjects the question is not so much one of politics or philanthropy, as of religion. In the eyes of the orthodox Mussulmans, the Sultan is not merely the Commander of the Faithful throughout the Mahommedan world, he is also the representative of the wide conquests and once glorious traditions of Islam, the embodiment of the earthly supremacy of the faith in which Moslems live and die. It is as if the Popes had been able to make themselves the political as well as the local successors of the Cæsars, and had united to their sacred character the authority of the Roman Emperor."

Sir Henry Layard expressed it still more forcibly in his despatch of June 19th, 1877, "That policy was partly based upon the belief that Turkey is a barrier to the ambitious designs of Russia in the East, and that the Sultan, the acknowledged head of the Mahommedan Faith, is a useful if not necessary ally to England, which has millions of Mussulmans amongst her subjects. He may be deprived of his empire, and may be reduced to the condition of a fifth rate Asiatic Potentate; but he will still be the Caliph of Islam, and the Mussulman world, in a struggle for very existence, may turn upon England as the principal cause of the danger that threatens it. Some persons, not without authority, are, I am aware, disposed to treat this consideration lightly; but I am persuaded from what I see passing around me, and from what I have learnt, that it is one which we ought seriously to bear in mind."

But there is, I am told, a fallacy involved in this

reasoning; and that the Sultan is only the head of the Mahommedan Faith because he is in possession of Mecca; and that if, at any time, he were to lose Constantinople and retain Mecca he would still be the Caliph of Islam, but that if he were to retain Constantinople and lose Mecca he would be so no longer. There have been several different Caliphates and no existing Mahommedan Sovereign can with any reason assert that he is the direct spiritual successor or "Caliph" of Mahommed—for the line of his successors was broken directly after his death, —the Shiahs cursing the first three Caliphs as intruders into the place of Ali—and it has been constantly broken since. The claim of the Sultan of Constantinople is based upon the fact that in 1481 the Egyptian Caliph gave up his dignity in favour of the Sultan Selim, the Conqueror of Egypt and Syria, and that the Shareef of Mecca thereupon did homage to him, and sent him the keys of the Caaba, upon the possession of which, as I have already explained, his title to be Caliph mainly depends. Now the Shareef of Mecca is at the present moment practically independent of the Sultan, and could at any moment if he chose, throw off allegiance to him and in that case the Sultan would infallibly lose his position as the spiritual head of Islam.

Indeed it is not improbable that on the inevitable break up of the Ottoman Caliphate this will occur. But in any case no such inviolable sanctity attaches to the person of the Caliph as the argument supposes. There have been various Mahommedan revolts against his authority, and the feeling in Bosnia, at the present time, is very strong against him. It is true that the Bosnian Mahommedans are incensed against the Armenians, whom they look upon as rebellious infidels, but they are equally indignant with the Sultan for the discredit he has brought upon their religion, and upon Mahommedans all over the world. They have always been loath to submit to being governed from Constantinople, and in 1831, Hussein Aga Berberli, "the Dragon of Bosnia," raised a rebellion against Mahomed II., whom he called the "Giaour Sultan," because that Sultan wished to abolish the janissaries, and to introduce various needful reforms. Almost all the Bosnian Begs flocked to his standard, and he was joined by Mustapha Pasha with twenty thousand revolted Albanians. In a short time he had conquered the whole of Bulgaria, and the greater part of Roumelia, and it is not unlikely that he would have taken Constantinople itself had he not quarrelled with Mustapha Pasha, and owing to their dissensions the Turkish Commander, Reshid Pasha, was enabled to attack and conquer each of them separately.

At this very moment the Young Turkish party are endeavouring to arouse a similar rebellion against the present Sultan. Members of that party are every day being arrested in Constantinople, and those who have been fortunate enough to escape have issued this appeal :—

"BRUSSELS, *June* 8, 1896.

" To all nations we send a warning begging them not to be misled by the wiles of the Turkish Government. Once again we implore the ministers who advise the monarchs of Europe to stay the hands of the murderers in Crete who are a disgrace to Mahomet and to the Turkish name.

"We who are exiled from our homes breathe liberty in free lands, and our hope is to arouse the sympathy of humanity on behalf of the many thousands who are in the clutches of the monsters who defy and insult the Powers of Europe through the mouths of the Turkish Diplomatists at foreign Courts.

"Already in the Asiatic provinces the world has witnessed scenes of organised carnage unparalleled in modern times. Before it is too late we warn the people of Europe that the Sultan has given explicit commands to the Governor of Crete 'to spare no rebel.' This means outrage and murder on the most extensive scale, and to effectively assist in the operations, troops, whose pay is in arrear many months, have been, and are being, despatched to Crete for the purpose of paying themselves by looting. Whilst the plotters of death are at work you are being deceived by false promises and reports, without a show of truth in them, imposed upon the

Press in all countries by the Sultan. We now solemnly ask, When will the despot, Abdul Hamid, be deposed by outraged Europe and his corps of assassins scattered, and a groaning people released from tyranny? Is the work of destruction of Moslem and Christian lives to continue unheeded? Are the inhuman barbarities by fire and sword of the treacherous Sultan, Abdul Hamid, to go on for ever?

"KHALIL ZIA, Secretary."

And in the face of this appeal, the article in the *Times*, from which I have just quoted, tries to stem the tide of feeling against the Sultan by urging that danger will be caused in India by denunciations of the Sultan in England.

"To most Englishmen, with a sense of self-respect and a just regard for the national dignity, it must seem unworthy of a great people to hoot as 'an assassin' and 'ruffian' a Sovereign whom our Government professes to consider a friend. To the Indian Mussulmans it seems scandalous. They can understand the abuse of a declared enemy. What they cannot comprehend is that we should be addressing the Sultan at Constantinople in terms of polite remonstrance, and reviling him in England in terms of the grossest insult.

"The Indian Mahommedan newspapers which have reached this country during the past months have gone through an ascending scale of protest, recrimination, and fierce menace, rising almost to threats. This conversion of a great and powerful community, late among the most loyal subjects of the Queen, into angry malcontents, has been viewed with concern by those responsible for the welfare of India. A correspondent, whose position entitles his opinion to much weight, forwards to us a collection of articles from representative journals of the Indian Mussulmans. 'Their feeling,' he says, in summarising the bulky packet, 'is one of the most intense irritation. That the Commander of the Faithful, the one Mahommedan Power able to treat on equal terms with the sovereigns of modern Europe, should be assailed with the foulest abuse, should be called a butcher and a murderer, is to them at once an outrage and a sacrilege.'"

But the question at issue is, not the effect that is being or may be produced in India, by calling the Sultan an assassin, but whether he is in reality an assassin; and if he be an assassin, whether it is right that the English Government should still profess, as this article says it does, to consider him as a friend.

The *Times* itself does not hold its correspondent's views, for in a leading article on the 16th September, 1876, this passage occurs:—"It is somewhat more instructive to hear that the Cabinet is not afraid to do what may offend the Mahommedans of Turkey, lest it should stir up anger among our Mahommedan subjects in India. The Chancellor of the Exchequer

(Sir Stafford Northcote) never heard "a more extraordinary doctrine, or one that he more completely repudiates," and the *Times* adds :—" Some advocates will not thank him for repudiating a doctrine which has filled a large place in their arguments." [1]

Moreover, the danger, if danger there be, applies with equal force to Russia, which is almost as great a Mahommedan Power as we are, and how little she regards it is shown by the fact that the Russian regiments, which were encamped next to Constantinople at the time of the Treaty of San Stefano, were largely composed of Mahommedan Cossacks; and of their loyalty there was never any question.

[1] Since this was written Mr. C. Disraeli, in moving an amendment to the Address, referred to the effect produced upon the Mahommedan subjects of the Queen by the change in English policy, and Sir E. Ashmead-Bartlett said that by such a policy we incurred the grave danger of irritating some seventy millions of her Majesty's Mussulman subjects, while the inevitable tendency of it would be to drive the Sultan more and more under the influence of Russia. Mr. Curzon replied much as Sir Stafford Northcote did in 1876. " He (Mr. C. Disraeli) deprecated," he said, " what he described as a policy of coercion of the Sultan, mainly on the ground of the consternation that it was producing or would produce among the Mahommedan inhabitants of the Indian Empire of her Majesty. I have had, perhaps, as many opportunities as the hon. member of studying this question, and I have had no evidence before me that any such consternation either already exists or is likely to be called into existence. Anyhow, whether that be so or not, I would submit to the House that our policy in Europe in discharge of the responsibilities which by treaty and otherwise we have on many occasions assumed, ought not to be dictated by considerations of the effect that policy may produce upon the inhabitants of her Majesty's Empire in India."

Nor should it be forgotten that a considerable number of the Indian Mahommedans are Shiahs like the Persians, and not Sunnis like the Turks, and that they not only do not acknowledge the Sultan as Caliph of Islam, but regard him and all Sunnis with the bitterest hatred; the feud between the two sects being so deadly, that it used to be declared by the Sunni Muftis to be more meritorious to kill one Shiah than to kill seventy Christians. Moreover, if it be so vital to our rule in India that we should maintain friendly relations with the Sultan, how is it that the Indian Mutiny, in which our bitterest opponents were Mahommedans, broke out within a year from the Crimean War, in which we had been allied with the Sultan and fighting side by side with the Turks. What is far more to be feared in India is that our inaction should be put down to fear—and that the natives, credulous and ready to believe any story however absurd, should believe that the Queen Empress, a Christian herself, has been obliged to stand by, an unwilling witness of the massacre of Christians, because the Sultan, the Padishah, is powerful enough to compel her to do so. Any one who knows the Asiatic character will agree that we are more likely to lose prestige by inaction in this matter, than by action, however vigorous.

But while I am on the subject of the Indian Mahommedans I will advert briefly to a matter which concerns them more nearly—the treatment habitually accorded to the Ghazis on our north-west frontier. A feeling of smouldering anger, a bitter memory cherished for the hour of retribution, is more likely to be aroused by the manner of the punishment meted out to them, than by any action it may be deemed necessary to take against the Sultan.

A Ghazi, I should explain, is a man who dedicates himself to death, and goes forth to slay the enemies of God until he is himself slain, believing that he will then be instantly taken up into Heaven. Now a Mahommedan believes in a material resurrection—that he will rise again in his actual body as he lived—and in order to stop the continual assassinations by these religious fanatics, the customary punishment on the north-west frontier is to hang the assassin and to burn his body afterwards, in order that the object for which he committed his crime may be defeated, and that no shrine may be raised over his body to act as a focus of disaffection. To hang him, it is argued, would be to reward him, by sending him at once to the Paradise he is seeking. But if he is burnt his aim is frustrated, for he believes that he cannot rise again if he has no body to rise with. In Egypt this superstitious anxiety for the entirety of the body is so strong, that if a man in hospital has a limb amputated it is given to him to be embalmed, in order that it may be buried with him when he dies. In our wars in that country burning is never resorted to, and though it is a debatable question whether it is advisable in India in times of peace, with the object of checking cowardly murders of unarmed and unsuspecting people, it is deeply to be regretted that it should be made use of in any of our frontier wars, for it is eminently calculated to produce a wide-spread resentment. It is religious insult of the worst kind, and worse than that, in Mahommedan eyes, it is an avowed and intended annihilation of the soul.

There are many men in India who revolt from it, and there are others who uphold it on the ground that it produces a wholesome feeling of terror—*oderint dum metuant;*—but it is not by such means, that we can hope to win the permanent attachment of the people, and some day such measures may recoil upon our own heads. The blood of the martyrs calleth from the ground, and punishments of this kind are more likely to produce a religious ferment than any sentimental feeling for the Caliph of Islam. It is idle to imagine that these things are not taken notice of by Mahommedans outside India. The editor of a Turkish paper in Bosnia, showed me an article commenting bitterly, though it seemed to me quite without reason, on the way in which Mahommedan troops are employed against Mahommedans in our frontier wars. This shows that what is being done in India is watched by Mahommedans elsewhere far more closely than we are apt to suppose.

We know little of what goes on beneath the surface of Eastern life, and a much less thing—the greasing of the cartridges—is generally credited with having been a main incentive to the Mutiny; and one of the most important lessons that the mutiny has taught us, is, as Lord Roberts has told us, that we should never do anything that can possibly be interpreted by the natives into disregard for their various forms of religion.

The cruelties committed by the Turks in their attempt to suppress the revolt in Bosnia and the Hercegovina were so great, and the ferment produced in the neighbouring Slav States was of so dangerous a character, that, anxious though England was to maintain the integrity of the Ottoman Empire, it was impossible for her to oppose the occupation of the country by Austria for the restoration of order. More than 200,000 fugitives fled across the Dalmatian, Serbian and Montenegrin frontiers. They suffered so terribly from pestilence, famine, and the rigour of the climate, that more than 90,000 of them perished during the three years that elapsed from the beginning of the insurrection to the occupation of the country by the Austrian troops. It was impossible that this state of things could be allowed to continue; moreover, it suited the purpose both of England and of Germany, that Austria should be allowed to take possession of these Provinces in order that she might act as a check upon any further extension of Russian influence in that direction; so by the terms of the Congress of Berlin, Bosnia, the Lion that guarded Stamboul, as the Turks called it, was made over to her for the enforcement of good government. How effectually the Austrians have performed the difficult task entrusted to them may be judged by the fact that though they have the three frontiers to defend of Serbia, Montenegro, and Turkey, their garrison consists only of 22,000 troops, aided by 2,500 military police.

Contrast this with the present condition of Macedonia, bearing in mind that by the Treaty of San Stefano the greater part of Macedonia was assigned to Bulgaria, but that England, under threat of war, compelled the provisions of that Treaty to be referred to a Congress of the Powers at Berlin, by whom it was retained under the Ottoman domination; the Powers being satisfied with the mere promise of the Porte, unsupported by any practical guarantee, of a reform in the administration, and of a more liberal treatment of the Christian populations throughout Turkey. How that promise has been kept in Crete and in Armenia the recent disturbances have enabled us to judge. Macedonia has not aroused so much sympathy, but her state is really worse, her population being more mixed than that of Crete, and therefore less able to combine. The country is in almost absolute anarchy. The troops are in a state of semi-mutiny, owing to not being regularly paid, and there is no security anywhere for either the life or the property of the rayahs. It is safe to travel in the Sandjak of Novi Bazar as far as Plevlje, to which point the Austrian troops extend, but beyond that it is dangerous to proceed without an escort. I was anxious to pass through it to Mitrovica, and from there to go by train to Salonica, but was told that the danger was too great.

Salonica is the natural outlet for the trade of the Balkan States, and ought to be a thriving port, but to reach it Macedonia must be traversed, and Macedonia is perilous to travel through even by rail. Only two years ago the express train was stopped by brigands, and the passengers held to ransom, and for some time after that most foreigners having business at Salonica preferred to get to it by sea from Marseilles, rather than run the risk of a similar misadventure. The proclamation issued this summer by the authorities at Prisrend, through which the railway passes, that it was dangerous for travellers to go outside the town, shows how disturbed a state the country is in. The better class of Turks would welcome the restoration of order, but they are powerless to restrain the riff-raff of the population and the licentious soldiery who are quartered there, and who are often directly incited and encouraged by the officials sent up by the Porte; and those horrors are daily enacted, which must always be enacted when a mob or undisciplined troops get the upper hand. Hardly any European dares to venture into it, and nothing certain is known of what is going on. We can only guess at what is likely to be done, by what we know is being done in the other provinces of Turkey. The people are too crushed, and are of too many jarring nationalities for any hope to be entertained of their being able to make a successful stand against their oppressors, and their only chance of freedom is through the action of the Powers. Every year that this is put off adds to the number of the victims, for there is a terrible truth in the Bosnian saying,

" Gdje su Turci, tu su i Vuci."

"Where the Turks are, there will also be the wolves."

CHAPTER XVIII

INEXPEDIENCY OF ISOLATED INTERVENTION ON BEHALF OF ARMENIA—DOES THE RETENTION OF CYPRUS AFFECT THE PRESENT SITUATION IN CONSTANTINOPLE?

WHAT is required is not the isolated intervention of England to coerce Turkey, but the abstention of England from intervention on behalf of Turkey. But for our intervention in the past the subject populations would long ere this have won their freedom for themselves, and many terrible massacres would not have taken place. Armenia has proved how true were Dr. Sandwith's words, uttered in 1876, "*I venture to predict there will be other, and infernal massacres, before England will yield to the just demands of Russia.*" And in another letter written from Serbia about the same time, he says, "Nothing to my mind is so utterly ignoble as the spirit of low jealousy towards Russia under the circumstances. It has doubtless intimidated the Czar Alexander, and added indefinitely to the horrors perpetrated in Turkey. The massacres of Bulgaria and Bosnia were the fruit of it; the crowds of naked and dying fugitives owe their sad fate to it." So, too, do the victims in the terrible massacres of the last two years, for by the 16th clause of the Treaty of San Stefano it is clear that it was the intention of Russia to remain in possession of Armenia, the greater part of which was at that time occupied by her troops, until she had satisfied herself that the needful reforms had been actually carried out, and not merely promised. That intention was frustrated by the Congress of Berlin, and Armenia abandoned to the fate which has since befallen it; England, by the Anglo-Turkish Convention, transferring to herself the responsibility for these reforms in return for Cyprus, and undertaking on her part to defend Armenia against Russian attack. There can be no doubt it is Russia which has prevented anything being done to protect the Armenians *now*; but it ought not to be forgotten that if she had had her way in 1878, the present situation would not have arisen; and that it was due to England that she did not have her way.

Except to arouse public opinion, it is of little use to hold excited meetings on behalf of the Armenians until we have convinced the European Powers that we are sincere in our professions of disinterestedness, and that we are really not desirous of any further acquisitions of territory. It is not as if the Armenian massacres were the first that had taken place, or that a feeling of horror had been aroused in England against the Turks. But that feeling of horror has always been transient, and has invariably disappeared when it was thought that action against Turkey, or rather inaction against Russia, would be against our imaginary interests. The massacre of Scio, in 1822, was more terrible and more uncalled for than those in Bulgaria, or than the recent massacres in Armenia. How atrocious it was, may be judged by the description given of it by Cobden. It is to be found in Mr. Morley's *Life of Cobden*, but I give it here, because I am anxious to emphasise the evanescent nature of our recurrent outbursts of indignation.

"Scio is an island about double the size of the Isle of Wight, like it presenting to the side of the open sea a wall of precipitous rocks, and offering to the spectator, who sails along the narrow strait which separates it from the mainland, a series of sloping hills and picturesque valleys. This island, with a population of upwards of a hundred thousand Greeks, was a kind of appanage of the Sultana Mother; and although ruled nominally by a Governor, and a garrison of two or three hundred Turks, the latter were in fact treated rather as their guests than their masters, and the inhabitants governed themselves by their own laws. Scio became the garden of the Archipelago; the wealthy Greeks retired there after a successful life of commerce, thither the aged and timid flocked for security; and the widow and orphan, that they might enjoy the protection and means of instruction, which no part of their enslaved country afforded. There too, was congregated all that was refined, intelligent and captivating of Greek society —the very name of Sciot, when applied to females, implied fascination and beauty. To complete the picture, schools, colleges, and libraries were established in this happy island. Such were the fruits of exemption from Turkish visitation. The dismal reverse of this picture remains to be told. Upon the breaking out of the Greek revolution the Sciots, conscious of their defenceless situation, renounced all participation in the plans of the insurgents, and the heads of their church and a number of the principal inhabitants voluntarily became hostages for the good conduct of their fellow citizens. The struggle between the Mussulman and the Christian—the tyrant and the slave, became a religous war; and the hapless inhabitants of Scio were at length given over by a mandate from Constantinople to the fanaticism of the faithful. There was immediately a rush from the capital, and from the large towns on the coast of Asia Minor towards Tehesme, the nearest point of embarkation to Scio. One cannot better picture the horrors that followed than by imagining that the Isle of Wight, with its happy and cultivated population, were suddenly given over to the lawless violence of 50,000 of the most desperate characters of London, Portsmouth, Southampton, and other large towns of the south, armed with knives, pistols, and guns. Imagine the worst that could arise from the unbridled cruelty and lust of such a mass ; imagine fields covered with wounded fugitives, streets filled with mangled corpses, the churches heaped with slain, and the rooms of every mansion and villa, from the nursery to the kitchen reeking with the blood of men, women and children. Not one house, excepting those belonging to the Consuls, escaped destruction. Fire, sword, and the still more deadly passions of fanaticism and lust ravaged the island for three months, during which such horrors were enacted—related to me by eye witnesses—as quite mock all human credulity. Of 100,000 inhabitants, not 5,000 were left alive upon the island. 40,000 of both sexes were sold into slavery, and the harems of Turkey, of Asia, and Africa are still filled with the female victims. Such was the massacre of Scio, unparalleled in modern history (a tragedy compared by the British Consul, an eye witness, to the destruction of Jerusalem), which thrilled the public mind of Europe and America with horror,"

And yet, after this massacre, we allied ourselves with Turkey in the Crimean War.

And to take a more recent instance : the agitation caused in England by the Bulgarian atrocities was in every way as vehement, and as sincere, as the present agitation, but within a very short time the rebound of feeling was so great that the people who had been so loud in the expression of their horror for the conduct of the Turks, were shouting that they had fought the Bear before, and would fight the Bear again, and the Cabinet felt strong enough to conclude a defensive alliance with Turkey, and to obtain possession of Cyprus. It is true that at the present time there is an almost universal feeling of revulsion against the Turks, but it is quite probable that this revulsion, genuine though it undoubtedly is, may be followed by an anti-Russian reaction, similar to that which followed the revulsion against them caused by the massacres in Scio and Bulgaria. That at least, is the opinion abroad, and it is difficult to say that it is not warranted by what has taken place in the past. Indeed signs are not wanting that this reaction is already setting in.

Sir Edward Clarke said quite lately, "It had become rather a popular thing to say that Lord Salisbury and the Government of the day had disavowed and departed from our traditional policy with regard to Turkey, and that Lord Salisbury had repudiated the policy of Lord Beaconsfield in this matter. That was an entire delusion. Lord Salisbury had never repudiated the policy of Lord Beaconsfield, and was not in the least likely to do so."

But Lord Salisbury's recent utterances are very little in accord with that policy, and, moreover, there are many members of the present Unionist Government who were its bitter opponents, and it is to be hoped that the pressure of other motives will not make them now accede to it.

Mr. Balfour said in one of his recent speeches, "We

all know, every man in England knows, that whether the Armenian agitation was taken up by one side or the other, by this statesman or that, it has never had for its object the acquisition of foreign territory, of further influence for England; and the fact that Europe has failed to recognise that has been a misfortune, not merely for Armenia, but in a less degree for this country, and for Europe itself." And he adds, by way of explanation, "But have we done nothing to deserve, to bring about this misfortune? Is it so easy for foreigners to understand what we say? I think not, and the reason I think not, is that I find it hard myself to understand some of the things which are done and said by gentlemen connected with politics,—with party politics,—in England."

But is not the reason which makes it so hard for them to understand us, rather what England, as a Power, has done, and the territory she has acquired, than anything that has been done or said by mere party politicians. It is deeds and not words, that leave a permanent impression, and one that is hard to eradicate. Few of those whom I met this summer in Bosnia think that England is honest in her present attitude. They believe that under cover of it she wishes to divert attention from her advance in Egypt, or that she wishes to acquire Crete. I was asked by an Austrian quite gravely one day why England had not taken Crete. I replied that I did not think any one in England had ever wished to take it; but I find in a letter from Mr. Bosworth Smith to the *Times*, dated February 22nd, 1877, the following passage which shows that my Austrian friend had some justification for his remark. "Occupy Crete! It is true indeed that such an occupation would be one of the measures which an important party in this country has long been recommending as a security to ourselves, but whatever our motives, it will be interpreted by all the Mediterranean States, nay by the whole of Europe, as an act of unscrupulous greed on the part of a Power which is already accused of pushing to an extreme its rights in that distant sea."

We did not occupy Crete, but we did occupy Cyprus; and it was, and is, regarded on the Continent as an act of unscrupulous greed, as indeed it was. Nay, it was more than that, for if we are to accept the inference drawn by the Duke of Argyll, it was the price of broken faith. "What lay behind the scenes, we know only in part; but this part is quite enough to throw a very unpleasant light on the probable motives of the Government. Dates go far to prove that they deserted and betrayed the cause of Greece, because they sold it to the Turks as part of the price to be paid for the Island of Cyprus." (Eastern Question, Vol. II, p. 170.) If this be so, when it becomes a question of the partition of Macedonia England is surely bound to insist that its Greek Provinces shall be assigned to Greece.[1] Is it to be

[1] And to refrain now from injuring Greece in Crete.

wondered at that our present professions should be received with incredulity, and that if we were to attempt to send our fleet to Constantinople, we should be deemed to be acting for our own interests and not for those of the Armenians, and that the result would be war? "I do believe," Lord Rosebery said, "that there was a fixed and resolute agreement on the part of the Great Powers of Europe—of all of them, or nearly all of them—to resist by force any single-handed intervention by England in the affairs of the East." I do not think many people who have been in Eastern Europe this summer can have much doubt of the truth of this belief.

Active intervention may be impolitic, and indeed impossible, but we can at least cause it to be clearly understood that, come what will, we will never again intervene in the interests of Turkey, but will leave her to deal, unassisted by us, with her insurgent Provinces, and with such of the Powers as may be willing to go to their assistance.

And though the present deadlock in Constantinople is the outcome of our policy in the past, there is no ground for believing that the position could be bettered, or that any useful end could be attained either by abandoning Cyprus, or by retiring from Egypt. It is quite clear that Russia has put forward these two questions now, as well as the Anglo-Turkish Convention, merely as an excuse to enable her to prevent any re-opening of the Eastern

Question at a time inconvenient to herself. However much we may have stood in her way in 1878, it is not England who is her chief opponent now, but Austria; and whether we remain in Cyprus or in Egypt, will not affect her attitude to that Power, or alter in any material way the present aspect of the situation.

Moreover, in Cyprus, as in Egypt, we have taken upon ourselves responsibilities which we cannot in honour shake lightly off because the island has become a charge upon us and a political incubus; we can, however, and we ought, to treat it in a very different manner.

We took possession of it at the same time that Austria took over Bosnia and the Hercegovina, and it is humiliating to contrast what she has done there with what we have done in Cyprus. I had a long conversation with an Austrian officer, who had been several times both there and in Egypt, and it was interesting to learn the impression produced upon a perfectly impartial witness (for the Austrians have always had a friendly feeling for the English) by what we have done in both places. "I don't think," he said, "that the people in Cyprus are either contented or prosperous. England has done scarcely anything for the island. She has not made a single railroad or opened it up in any way, and the taxation is frightful. She is not able to do anything, for she has no money to do it with; but that is due to the terms under which she took it over. When Austria occupied Bosnia and the Hercegovina, she not only stipulated that she should have no yearly payment to make to Turkey, but also that those Provinces should not be liable for any portion of the Turkish debt, so that the whole of their revenues might be available for their internal improvement. England was so desirous to have Cyprus that she agreed that the island should pay a large yearly tribute to Turkey, and it was subsequently arranged that the tribute should be paid not to the Porte, but to the Turkish bondholders. In fact she constituted herself a far more efficient tax collector for the bondholders than Turkey would have been. The island is fertile, and in old days was exceedingly wealthy. You govern well and justly I admit, but the country can never become prosperous so long as it is saddled with this enormous charge. In Egypt, on the other hand, you have done really magnificent work. You have not only made the country commercially more prosperous, but you have greatly bettered the condition of the fellaheen, and looking to their interests alone it would be a pity if you gave it up."

This candid opinion of the crushing nature of our taxation is fully confirmed by the statement made by Mr. Browne, in his recent article upon "England's duty to Cyprus," that while in Crete the average annual amount paid in taxation directly and indirectly per head of the population is fourteen shillings, in Cyprus it exceeds twenty-six shillings, and it cannot be otherwise with the enormous tribute to meet every year of £92,000, which is paid not to the Sultan, but to the British Treasury on behalf of the bondholders of the four per cent. loan to Turkey of 1855, which was guaranteed by both England and France.

But Mr. Browne has told us of another matter which will exercise a still greater influence than oppressive taxation upon the future well-being of the island.

In discussing the suggestion that it should be handed over to Greece, he represents the Mahommedans as speaking thus:—"We Mussulmans are a minority (and words like these are not forgotten or misunderstood by those who hear them), but we are warriors from of old, and would have with us, almost to a man, the troopers and zaptiehs who constitute the only native armed and disciplined force, and you may be certain that we would die to the last man, and fight to the last gasp, rather than submit to Greek supremacy."

Now the Turks always talk like that, but when the time comes they do not die to the last man. They fight bravely till they are fairly beaten, and then they settle quietly down, and become peaceable, law-abiding people. They did not resist us when we took possession of the island for they saw that resistance was useless; they said it was God's will, and submitted. They would equally submit to the Greeks, if they were compelled to do so.

They used precisely the same language in Bosnia during the insurrection. This is what one of them said to Mr. Arthur Evans: " Rather than submit to that," he replied, "if that is what is meant by the new Constitution, we will shut ourselves up in our houses, with our wives and our children, and with our own hands we will slay our wives and our children, and last of all we will cut our own throats with our own handjars"; and Mr. Evans adds, "There is something grand and terrible in this Essene-like resolution of fanaticism which must at least command respect. For these are not idle words. I do not doubt that in certain eventualities some at least of the leading Mahommedans of Bosnia are prepared to carry them into effect. Yet Allah is great, and 'Kismet' greater, and Children of the Prophet not less fanatical have before now bowed their heads to the irresistible decrees of fate. Were it once conclusively demonstrated to the Begs and other Bosnian fanatics that destiny was against them, without doubt the large majority would submit to force majeure." And as a matter of fact they did so. They fought desperately, until they saw that the struggle was hopeless, and then accepted patiently what they felt to be inevitable. And the same thing has often occurred in India. We are always being told we must not meddle with the Turks because they are a very desperate people when driven to bay; but it is better to grasp a nettle boldly than to live in perpetual dread of it, to have a brief though bloody campaign like that in Bosnia, to be followed afterwards by security and peace.

What is, however, of more direct concern to England is this: why should the troopers and zaptiehs who constitute the only native armed force be almost to a man with the Mussulmans? Why have we left it in the power of the Turks to work such mischief? The cost that it would have entailed has prohibited the creation of a corps of English police similar to the Austrian gendarmerie corps in Bosnia and the Hercegovina, but, in the corps of native police which we have been obliged to employ, why have we almost entirely enlisted Turks? Why have we not taken the down-trodden Greeks by the hand and made men of them so that they may be able to defend themselves if the necessity for it should arise? Why have we not tried to teach them how to govern their own country in the way the Russians did in Rumelia, to which the Marquis of Bath has borne such eloquent testimony.

"The Governor, Prince Dondoukoff Korsakoff, devoted himself with entire singleness of purpose and oblivious of the interests (certainly in the narrower sense) of his own country, to the creation of a national life and a political organisation among this hitherto down-trodden people. He found everything in confusion; he introduced order and formed an administration. This administration, it is true, he put under Russian officials, but he based it on the municipal and communal system, by means of which, apart from Turkish laws and officials, the Bulgarians had managed their own affairs ; and thus he incorporated into it the most intelligent and leading men amongst them.

"When the Russians withdrew in June, 1879, there was no difficulty in supplying their place by Bulgarians who had acquired some amount of administrative experience. . . . But he did more than all this. Together with the sentiment of national independence, he strove successfully to infuse into the minds of the people a feeling of personal self-respect and self-confidence. I met at his table Bulgarian officers who, but a few months before had been simple peasants, and who were received on equal terms with the highest Russian officials.

.   .   .   .   .

When he surrendered his authority to the elected Prince, he handed over to him an army, an administration, above all a self-confident and well-ordered people."

Why have we not done something of the same kind in Cyprus? Wherever we have dependencies (as distinguished from Colonies) we govern well and justly—that all men own. But we do not create a national sentiment—we do all we can to suppress it. In India this constitutes at once our strength and our weakness. It is the fact that we are purely *alien rulers* that enables us to balance and control the opposing forces of the Mahommedans and the

Hindus, but it also entails this consequence, that if at any time we were obliged to withdraw from the country we should leave the people in a state of anarchy, for we have made of ourselves the cement without which the whole administration will fall to pieces. In India that is an intelligible and a rational policy, because we propose to remain there so long as our swords will hold it for us. But in Cyprus the case is altogether different. We are bound to recognise the fact that our government of the island must be limited in duration. We ought, therefore, while it continues, to educate the people to govern themselves, so that when we retire we may, like Prince Dondoukoff Korsakoff, leave behind us "an army, an administration, above all, a self-confident and well-ordered people." And the first step towards that end is to rectify the unfair preponderance of Mahommedans in the police, for the Christian Greeks constitute three-fourths of the population and the Turks only one-fourth. That being so, if we retain it, we ought to place the Greek population in such a position that they may be able to take up the reins of government after us without any such danger of bloodshed as we have been warned of. That surely is our true duty to Cyprus.

CHAPTER XIX

PROBABILITY OF REVOLT IN MACEDONIA—IS ENGLAND'S ATTITUDE TO IT TO BE ONE OF SYMPATHY, OR OF DISCOURAGEMENT?

So far as Armenia is concerned it is clear that our hands are tied, and that isolated intervention is impracticable. But when Macedonia takes the place of Armenia we shall be in a very different position. There will be no question then of forcing the Dardanelles, for Macedonia is on this side of them, and has an extensive seaboard upon which our fleet can operate. Every day the question of Macedonia is becoming more insistent, and the necessity for action more urgent. The conditions of life there have become so unbearable that in spite of the apparent futility of revolt, bands of insurgents have collected in the mountains much as they did in the beginning of the insurrection in Bosnia. Turkish troops have been sent out to disperse them, and orders have been given by the Sultan that they shall be treated with the utmost severity. A *Times* telegram from

Athens dated December 18th of last year states that :—

"The situation in Macedonia presents many disquieting features, and though comparative tranquillity may be maintained for the next few months there is every probability that events of no ordinary importance will take place in that country in the spring. The utmost secrecy is maintained with regard to the transactions of the revolutionary society known as the National Hetæria, but there can be little doubt that it has succeeded in raising considerable funds and is engaged in making energetic preparations for the coming struggle. The Macedonian committees in Bulgaria are also renewing their activity. The Turkish Government is fully conscious of the danger, and for some time past the military authorities in Macedonia have been engaged in concerting measures for the suppression of the anticipated revolt, while arms and ammunition are being distributed among the Mahommedan population."

The reports that come in day after day show that the country is practically in a state of anarchy.

The Greeks, the Serbs, and the Bulgarians are all eager to assist their fellow-countrymen, and are only held back from doing so by the efforts of their respective Governments. But when tyranny comes to a certain pitch Governments become powerless to restrain their subjects from acting in accordance with their sympathies. Before many months are over there is certain to be an organised uprising, and the insurgents will receive powerful assistance from without. Indeed the struggle has already begun. A Reuter's telegram from Athens, dated November 10th, 1896, reports that :—

"The insurgent band under the chief Lepelioti recently recrossed the frontier into Macedonia and on Saturday last gave battle to the Turkish troops at a spot three hours' distant from the border. The firing was distinctly heard in one of the Greek villages, the inhabitants of which assembled on the heights to watch the fighting. Heavy loss was sustained on both sides." And King Alexander of Serbia, in a recent speech, when referring to the condition of the Serbs in Macedonia used these words, "We must turn our eyes in that direction. There we must save our brothers."

Whether the insurrection will succeed or not will depend very much upon the attitude maintained towards it by the Powers; and it will furnish a much truer test than Armenia whether the change of feeling in England, with regard to Turkey and to our traditional policy in the Balkans, is sincere or not.

To prove that we have been sincere, it will not even be necessary for us to take direct action against Turkey; all that is required is that we should not go to her assistance, as we have always hitherto done. Some members of the present Government apparently advocate a continuance of the old policy of attempting to reform Turkey from within, by assisting the young Turkish party in their efforts to secure better government. But the one lesson that we ought by this time to have learnt, is that all projects of Turkish reform are illusory, and that improvement can only be effected from without and not from within—that, in fact, to put it bluntly, when mortification has set in, dissolution is inevitable. Carlyle's words have an even stronger application now than when they were written; and the truth of his surmise of the comparative easiness of the task of enforcing good government in the Turkish provinces has since been abundantly proved, both in Bulgaria and in Bosnia.

"Such immediate and summary expulsion of the Turk from Europe," he wrote, "may appear to many a too drastic remedy; but to my mind it is the only one of any real validity under the circumstances. Improved management of these unhappy countries might begin on the morrow after this long-continued curse was withdrawn, and the ground left free for wise and honest human effort. The peaceful Mongol inhabitants would of course be left in peace, and treated with perfect equity, and even friendly consideration; but the governing Turk, with all his Pashas and Bashi-Bazouks, should at once be ordered to disappear from Europe, and never to return. This result is in the long run inevitable, and it were better to set about it now than to temporise and haggle, in the vain hope of doing it cheaper some other time. As to the temporary or preparatory Government of the recovered provinces, cleared of their unspeakable Turkish Government for twenty, or say any other term of years, our own experiences in India prove that it is possible, and in a few faithful and skilful hands even easy."

The chief opponents to any change being made in Macedonia are Austria and Germany, who both have Russia pressing upon their frontiers, and who both dread a further extension of her influence in the Balkans. Austria, moreover, is credited with a desire to obtain Macedonia for herself, or at any rate that portion of it which extends from the Sandjak of Novi Bazar to Salonica, and it is perfectly true that those who belong to the forward school, especially if they are Croats, are anxious for a further advance in that direction. One of them told me frankly that he hoped to have a Government post in Salonica before another year was out. But neither the German-Austrians nor the Hungarians wish to see the Slav element in the dual monarchy increased. They think it dangerously large already, and they see clearly that if they took possession of Macedonia, hemmed in as they would be between Serbia and Bulgaria on one side, and Montenegro on the other, and with Russia fomenting internal discontent, as she infallibly would, their position would be altogether untenable. Up to the present time their policy has been to maintain the *status quo*, for they naturally prefer to have on their frontiers a weak power like Turkey rather than a strong power like Russia, or an autonomous state under Russian influence. But there are signs that this policy is changing, and that they are beginning to perceive that as it is inevitable that Macedonia should be freed, it is wiser to make friends with the Macedonians than to force them into the arms of Russia. In Bosnia this change is markedly apparent. Less bitterness and distrust is shown of Serbia and Montenegro; the orthodox Serbs are treated in a far more liberal way than they used to be. To give the people a helping hand, rather than to discourage them in their coming struggle, would be for England, as well as for Austria, the wisest policy to pursue.

The Austrians (not the Magyars, who seem to have an enmity to the Serbs) are quite alive to the importance of creating a system of buffer states friendly to themselves; so much so, that in 1865 they even suggested that Prince Michael of Serbia should take possession of Bosnia as far as the Vrbas. They see clearly that if Russia once becomes dominant in Macedonia, she would not be satisfied with that, but would covet Dalmatia as well, and perhaps even Croatia, and to prevent so great an extension of her influence is a matter of life and death to Austria; it affects her very existence as a nation. Her safest course is to convince the people of these newly created states that their interest lies in looking to her for support rather than to Russia. Unfortunately up to the present she has persistently alienated them. Baron von Moltke, writing in 1829, makes this significant observation : "The worst was that it soon became manifest that the Greeks would secure their freedom without the intervention of European diplomacy ; and the moment this contingency appeared possible, there arose a vague feeling of distrust among the powers of Europe, lest some neighbour, forgetting the principle of non-intervention, might stretch forth the right hand of fellowship, and thus obtain lasting influence and great political importance." What happened then in Greece, and afterwards in Bulgaria, seems likely to happen in Macedonia now. The people are beginning to rise in disconnected bands, which can be easily put down by the Turkish troops, but if those troops should be guilty of the cruelties which have invariably accompanied the suppression of revolts in Turkey, it is impossible that the European powers can look supinely on, or, in any case, that Russia can do so.

With Armenia it was quite different, for Russia is the only power upon whose frontier Armenia touches ; and Russia is indifferent to the Armenians, because they are neither Slavs nor Orthodox Christians. In Macedonia, on the other hand, almost the whole of the population are Orthodox, and a large proportion of them are Slavs, and it will be as impossible to restrain the Russian people from sympathising with and assisting them, as it was in 1876 to hold them back from assisting in Bosnia, in Serbia, and in Bulgaria.

For whatever may be the motives that have influenced Russian statesmen, to the Russian people the cause of the oppressed Christians always has been and always will be a holy cause, and a war undertaken on their behalf becomes to them a veritable crusade. "Not to conquer," said the Grand Duke Nicholas to his men, "but to defend our down-trodden brethren, and to vindicate the faith of Christ do we go forth. Forward then; ours is a holy work, and God is with us."

What actuates them is not so much a wish for political aggrandisement as a genuine and natural desire to improve the condition of peoples allied to themselves by blood, and by the still more sacred tie of a common religion. And if we will only bear in mind the fact that the same language—the old Slavonic—is used both by the Russians and by the bulk of the Balkan Christians in the services of the Orthodox Church, so that a Serb or Bulgar can worship in Russia, or a Russian in Serbia, or Bulgaria, or Macedonia, and feel as though he were in his own country, it will make it clear not only that the Tzar Alexander was perfectly sincere in his statement that he undertook the war in order that the condition of the Christians in Turkey should be bettered, but that each succeeding Tzar and all Russia with him must be moved by the same desire.

"This state of things," said Prince Gortchakoff in his despatch of May, 1877, "and the acts of violence resulting from it, excite in Russia an agitation caused by the Christian feeling so profound in the Russian people, and by the ties of race and faith which unite them to a great part of the Christian population of Turkey."

What influences the Russians is in truth a higher feeling than the desire for mere political advantage which influences the other peoples of Europe, and for that reason it is inevitable that it is from their hands that these down-trodden races should look for their redemption.

But Russia, though she has shown herself their helper and liberator whilst they were in bondage, has also shown herself to be their most insidious foe when freed.

Alike in Bulgaria, in Serbia, and in Greece she is feared and dreaded by all who are jealous for the national independence and who do not wish their country to become merged in a greater Russia. For that reason they would gladly turn to Austria for support, because Austria being a Catholic country there is not the same danger of her obtaining an overmastering influence over the minds of the unthinking masses; and it is deeply to be regretted that Austria by her commercial policy, and by the oppressive control over the railway system of the Balkans which was given to her by the Congress of Berlin, and indeed by her general attitude of suspicious hostility, should have done all she can to estrange them. Her main object seems to have been to stave off as long as possible the change that must inevitably occur, and only last spring Count Goluchowsky urged the Bulgarian Government to restrain its subjects from helping the Macedonians, just as Metternich did all he could to assist the Sultan during the Greek war of independence. It is doubtful if Austria will maintain this attitude should the insurrection become serious, but she runs the danger by standing aloof for so long of alienating still further the Orthodox Slavs, and of throwing them once more into the arms of Russia. Her true policy, and the true policy of England, is to cut the ground from under Russia's feet by being beforehand with her in insisting that the country shall be freed, instead of waiting to be compelled by Russia to yield a grudging and ungracious assent to a freedom arranged by and won through her unsupported exertions. But if Austria should not be willing to depart from her former policy there is no reason why England should not, and if it were made clear that England and France, or even England alone, were willing to procure for Macedonia, not an illusory alteration for the better under constitutions to be set aside at the

Sultan's pleasure, or Christian governors to be dependent entirely upon his will, but a real deliverance from Turkey under some form of autonomous government (or if it should be deemed preferable, by a partition of the country between Bulgaria, Serbia, Greece, and Montenegro) it would be impossible for either Austria or Russia to resist what was proposed. They could only do so by acting together, of which there is not much likelihood, and in all probability they would see the wisdom of a cordial concurrence.

Owing to the variety of races inhabiting it, and to the jealousies and hatreds existing between them, it would be difficult, if not utterly impracticable, to form Macedonia into an independent state, and it will probably be deemed wiser to divide it between Bulgaria, Greece, Serbia, and Montenegro. But if such a partition should be effected, the fact should not be overlooked that Stara Serbia, and with it Salonica, should in justice be assigned to Serbia. It is true that Salonica is mainly Greek, and that even in the days of the Tzar Dushan it never belonged to Serbia, but the Serbian frontier was close beside it, and it was at that time the principal port for Serbian commerce. Greece is in no need of ports, and Bulgaria has Varna, but Serbia is absolutely landlocked, and in consequence is at the mercy of Austria with whom she has lately been obliged to conclude a stringent commercial treaty. If she had Salonica she would be able to develop a trade with other countries. As I have mentioned before, the Consular returns show that since the incorporation of Bosnia and the Hercegovina into the Customs union of Austria-Hungary, England has lost a trade of more than £400,000. That trade has gone beyond possibility of recall. Are we going now to lose our trade, present and prospective, with Serbia and with Macedonia also?

CHAPTER XX

IMPOSSIBILITY OF THE TURKS REFORMING, OR OF CESSATION OF MASSACRE—CHANGE OF ATTITUDE OF THE EUROPEAN POWERS—PROBABLE MOTIVES OF RUSSIA—THE NATURAL ALLY OF ENGLAND IS AUSTRIA—ADVISABILITY OF STRENGTHENING BOTH SERBIA AND GREECE

SOME members of the present Government seem disposed to cling to the device which has been so often found wanting, of retaining the disaffected provinces of Turkey under the rule of the Porte; merely endeavouring to secure for them better government by roseate constitutions and an improved gendarmerie. That is what is being done in Crete. It does not seem to be succeeding there. It has never succeeded well anywhere in Turkey, and no one who knows anything of the Turks believes that it ever will. Things have gone too far in Macedonia for any half-measures of that kind. The only thing that will satisfy the people is an entire deliverance. We can give them that if we will, for if England helps them, neither Russia nor Austria will dare to stand aside. England, moreover, has a right—indeed it is her duty to make the first move, in the same way that Canning made his appeal to the

Tzar in 1826 on behalf of the Greek insurgents—because it is she who is mainly responsible for their present condition. And by securing justice and freedom for this unhappy people whose misery is so largely due to ourselves, we shall not be damaging our own interests, but, shall in fact, be forwarding them; and more than that we shall be repairing so far as it is in our power to do so, the terrible harm that we have worked through our persistent interference in a question that we ought never to have meddled with.

"You talk to me," said Mr. Gladstone, in one of his great speeches at the time of the Bulgarian agitation, "of the established tradition with regard to Turkey. I appeal to the established tradition—older, wider, nobler far—a tradition, not which disregards British interests, but which teaches you to seek the promotion of these interests in obeying the dictates of honour and of justice." It is because England, as a nation, has fashioned her policy, taken as a whole, upon these principles, that she holds her present proud position.

An Austrian, talking to me about this very subject, expressed the same truth in a different way. "The English are a strange people," he said, "one never knows what they will do, or what their policy will be, because, if they are once convinced that a thing is right, and ought to be done, they are quite capable of insisting that it shall be done, even if it be contrary to their own interests."

To that sturdy independence of judgment, that refusal to have questions of national moment decided for us in accordance merely with diplomatic tradition our national greatness is due. And that independence of judgment was never more needed than when dealing with this question of the dismemberment of Turkey. Mr. Gladstone's disregarded words come back to us now with a solemnity increased by all that has occurred in Turkey since the day on which they were uttered.

"I beseech you to ponder these subjects in your hearts. Depend upon it there never was a time when the good fame of England was more completely at stake. If the incessant dinning into your ears of maintaining British interests, if the harbouring of every kind of suspicion against the general policy of Russia, if the abuse of these unhappy Christians, who having been an enslaved people, are necessarily in some respects subject to the demoralising results of slavery; if the recent invention of the Turkish Constitution—made to order, and intended to act as a bar thereby to the proposals of the Conference—if these or any other like devices —for I must say that the imagination of the Turkish press in this country is fertile beyond everything in manufacturing them—if we are going to be drawn aside by these from the great proposals we have in view, then we shall leave to posterity the melancholy lesson that the people of England, having long dwelt with an apathy due to an influence we all laboured under, and having once been awakened to a noble and gallant effort in favour of the principles of humanity, justice and freedom, were content to be lulled to sleep again by finding the task of duty too heavy for them to perform, and that it was more convenient for a man to go about his pursuits, his own money making, and his own pleasures, and to dismiss from his mind these painful and harrowing subjects. That may be so; but if that be true, these are the marks of a degenerate nation; this is the conduct which emphatically confutes the doctrine of human progress."

When the Eastern question assumes the acute phase that it must very shortly do, for the finances of Turkey are rotten, are we going to adopt a new and more generous policy? Or, moved as of old by an unreasoning dread of Russia, are we going to discount again the undoubted good we have done in India and in Egypt by continuing to work untellable mischief in Eastern Europe?

That will be the question for decision when Macedonia bursts into revolt.

And however loth certain members of his party may be to abandon what has been for so many years the traditional policy of England, it is evident that Lord Salisbury's patience is nearly at an end, and that he does not intend to have any further interference on behalf of the Turks. He has always doubted the capability of the Turks to reform, and in his recent despatch to Sir N. O'Conor he quoted significantly the words used by him in another despatch in 1878: "Whether use will be made of this—probably the last—opportunity which has thus been obtained for Turkey by the interposition of the Powers of Europe, and of England in particular, or whether it will be thrown away, will depend upon the sincerity with which Turkish statesmen address themselves to the duties of good government, and the task of reform." It is idle to hope that they will ever do this, and it is equally idle to hope that there will ever be a cessation of the liability to massacre. There cannot be, because to a Mahommedan the massacre of an infidel is not only not a crime, but is a religious obligation. It is true that the more humane amongst them deprecate a recourse to it, and that the Sheik-ul-Islam prohibited the softas from taking part in the recent massacre in Constantinople, but the fact remains, and will always be operative with the mass of Mahommedans, that it is inculcated by the Koran in precisely the same way that it was inculcated by the Old Testament. Just as Saul was bidden to smite the Amalekites, and to slay both man and woman, infant and suckling, ox and sheep, camel and ass, so the Koran bids the true believers attack the infidels with arms, and treat them with severity: "Their abode shall be hell, and an ill journey shall it be thither." This they are bidden to do because temptation to idolatry is more grievous than slaughter. Amongst Christian nations the Old Testament has been replaced by the more merciful law of Christ, but to the Mahommedans the Koran is still the one guide to conduct. It is this which makes it possible for a Christian government to deal equitably with its Mahommedan subjects, but which makes it impossible for a Mahommedan government to do otherwise than deal harshly with its Christian subjects. And there is no hope that time will effect any change for the better. The motives for oppression are too deep-seated for that. So long as the Christians submit patiently to everything that may be inflicted upon them, so long will they be permitted to live, but that permission may at any time be rightfully withdrawn. In the eyes of the Mahommedans they have justly forfeited their lives by their infidelity, and upon the least sign of revolt it becomes a religious duty to extirpate them utterly: "But whoso separateth himself from the Apostle, after true direction hath been manifested unto him, and followeth any other way than that of the true believers, we will cause him to obtain that to which he is inclined, and will cast him to be burned in hell, and an ill journey shall it be thither."

That what the Turks do is done in pursuance of what they conceive to be a religious duty, explains many puzzling inconsistencies between their conduct under ordinary circumstances, and their conduct when under the influence of fanatical passion. It may lessen the abhorrence we feel towards them, but it makes it all the more impossible that they should be allowed to exercise power any longer. Humane and excellent when under control, they have proved themselves quite unfit to be masters. They have withered like a blight every country of which they have taken possession.

"There was now an opportunity," said Lord Salisbury in 1858, "which might never recur, of supporting those very principles which we revered, of establishing those institutions to which we owed our own happiness, and of securing the freedom and welfare of thousands of our fellow-creatures. That opportunity had been afforded in consequence of a pledge given by ourselves, and if it should be neglected and thrown away, the responsibility would fall upon us, and all would feel that it had been lost by our betrayal and our falsehood."

Those words might well have been spoken at the present time.

Since this was written events have taken place in Crete which have brought into clear relief the changed attitude of the different Powers towards Turkey, and have shown beyond a doubt that the Power most anxious to maintain the Sultan is not England, but Russia; and that England has only taken part with reluctance in the coercive measures put in force against Greece. What has brought about Russia's change of front? In the Balkans the following reasons are generally given. It is known that two years ago she effected a secret treaty with Turkey, by which she undertook to uphold, if necessary by force, the Ottoman Empire as it at present exists. At first sight the alliance seems so unnatural that it is difficult to understand what motives can have induced her to enter into it, but the explanation that is given is intelligible enough. She foresees that some time during the next ten or twenty years terrible convulsions will probably occur in Western Europe, and that it will be greatly to her advantage to have Turkey, not as an enemy, but as an ally. Turkey, it is true, is financially broken down, but she has almost an unlimited supply of excellent fighting men, of whom Moltke said that, properly led, they would make the finest soldiers in the world. It is evident that in a war with Austria it would give her an almost overwhelming advantage to be able to attack Hungary in flank with Turkish troops, and to have the Balkans to fall back upon as a base of operations. Up to the present she has been able to reconcile her own subjects to her change of policy by the assurance that when the Great Slav Conquest has been effected, she will be in a position to settle the question of Turkey by herself without fear of outside intervention. That is perfectly true; but when she is in a position to do that, she will also be in a position to absorb the Balkan States into herself—a fate they have little wish should overtake them.

The alliance was put to the proof almost as soon as it was made, when England suggested that force should be used to put a stop to the massacres in

Armenia. Russia not only declined to accede to that proposal, but stated definitely that she would resist it by force. With the exception of France and England none of the Powers cared much about Armenia, and France gave way rather than endanger her newly-cemented friendship with Russia; and the Armenians being neither Slav nor Orthodox, little sympathy was felt for them by the Russians themselves. But now that insurrection has broken out in Crete, and may break out in Macedonia, Russia is in a very different position. She is bound to uphold the Sultan's authority in order to retain her hold upon the Turks, but by doing so she is in danger of losing her influence with the orthodox populations of the Balkans, and of producing a dangerous ferment amongst her own subjects. She is, therefore, most anxious that whatever action is taken should be the concerted action of the Powers, that the whole odium should not fall upon her; and it is believed that Germany (who at the present moment is doing all she can to detach Russia from France) in insisting that the severest possible measures should be enforced against Greece, is merely acting in compliance with a suggestion from St. Petersburg that it would be less objectionable for such a proposal to emanate from her than from Orthodox Russia. Presumably, she hopes to obtain a promise that in the event of a war between herself and France, Russia will hold aloof. The French are beginning to perceive this, and to chafe under the necessity of being consenting parties any longer to the Turkish massacres. As one of their papers observed, there seems little hope that Russia will help them to regain Alsace and Lorraine, and in taking part against Greece they are acting against their own natural sympathies. But of all the Powers Austria runs the greatest danger by permitting a continuance of the present state of affairs in the Balkans. She has produced order in Bosnia, but she has not made herself beloved; and has, therefore, not only not strengthened her position, but has materially weakened it. Her aim, and the aim of England, should be to hasten on the dissolution of European Turkey, not to retard it; to strengthen as much as possible Serbia and Greece, both of them countries with a strong national spirit, and both dreading the absorption by Russia that is already looming over them. For this reason an occupation of Crete by Austria would be a most suicidal measure. It would greatly increase the irritation already felt against her in many parts of the Balkans, an irritation she could do much to allay by coming forward now as the champion of the Christians. She is not strong enough to do this by herself, but the cordial co-operation of Austria, England, Serbia, and Greece would go far towards producing the desired equilibrium, and to freeing Macedonia, for, in the face of such a combination, Russia would hesitate to take active measures on behalf of the Sultan.

The difficulties that have arisen in the settlement

of Crete are far less than those that will arise in that of Macedonia, and Russia is doing all she can to prevent matters there from coming to a head. The Tzar has recently expressed, both to the Serbian and to the Bulgarian Governments, his strong personal disapproval of any intervention on behalf of the Macedonians. This, and the jealousy of each other's claims displayed by the Greeks, the Bulgarians, and the Serbs, may delay the insurrection for a time, but it must break out sooner or later. When it does break out will England and Austria assist in putting it down, or by helping the insurgents, will they throw upon Russia the onus of taking action as the declared supporter and ally of the Mahommedans, instead of the Christians as of old? In all probability she will shrink from doing that, and some arrangement will be come to by which Macedonia also may be delivered from Turkish rule. But if, on the other hand, she should deem it to her interest to go to war rather than consent to any further curtailment of Turkish territory, is England prepared to stand by the declarations she has made, and, as Lord Salisbury said last year at Dover, "to write her name again as the maintainer of civilization, as the friend of peace, but as the indomitable defender of the liberty of independent people, which has been her fame and her distinction." Lord Salisbury is known upon the Continent to be cautious in his declarations of policy, because he does not speak unless he is prepared, if necessary, to act up to his words. That this is so may enable him to procure a substantial measure of freedom for Macedonia without having recourse to war; but if that should prove to be impossible, and war to be a necessity, the nation will feel that it has not been undertaken lightly, but for the cause of justice and of honour.

INDEX

ADVANCES, by Government, to tenants for purchase of holdings, 40

Albanians, descendants of original Illyrians, 82

Animals, kind treatment inculcated by Mahommedan religion, 154

Appel, Baron, Governor of Bosnia, 16; feeling aroused by death of Baroness, 17

Argyll, Duke of, opinion of English attitude to the Bosnian Insurrection, 215; to the Balkan Christians in general, 217; and to Greece, 245

Armenia, Mahommedan view of the massacres, 221—223; responsibility of England, 239; difference between Armenia and Macedonia, 260—274

Austria, change of feeling in Bosnia, 16; Austrian policy in Bosnia, Dalmatia, and Servia, 100—104; in the Balkan States, 258—260, 263, 275, 276

Avars, 85

BALFOUR, speech by Right Hon. A. J., 244

Banjaluka, 116

Bath, Marquis of, opinion of Bulgaria, 217, 218; and of the Russian occupation of Eastern Rumelia, 251

Beaconsfield, Earl of, speech against Russia, 215

Beach, Sir M., Hicks-, speech on October 13th, 1896

Berberli, Hussein Aga, revolt of, 225

Bihać, 162

Bjelašnica, 27

Bogumiles, traces near Jablanica, 71; origin and tenets, 86

Bosnia, outline of history, 80—89; insurrection in, 214, 234

Bravska Planina, 146

Brčka, 182

Bright, speech by, Right Hon. John, 209

Brod, 12

CADIS, preside over separate courts for Mahommedans, 54—57; schools where they are trained, 57

Caliphate, whether Indian and other Mahommedans outside Turkey have any special reverence for Sultan as the Caliph of Islam, 222—231

Canning, despatch to Sir A. Paget, 211

Carlyle, letter from, 157

Catholics, hatred of Orthodox Greek Church, 31

Cattaro, 198

Cetina, source of river, 97

280 INDEX

Christianity, Introduction into Illyria, 84
Clarke, Sir E., speech by, 243
Cobden, description of massacre of Scio, 240
Colonists, Polish, 127, 128
Corpus Christi Day in Serajevo, 29
Crete, speech by Hon. George Curzon, 212; appeal on behalf of island by the young Turkish party, 227; letter from Mr. Bosworth Smith, 245; motives of Russian attitude to the insurgents and to Greece, 272—275
Croats, animosity to Orthodox Serbs, 31; origin of, 85; legend of creation of the different languages, 92; aspire to federation similar to that possessed by Hungary, 100; Agram, their political and literary centre, 120
Cvjetićanin, Colonel, 14, 76
Cyprus, 245—253
Cyrillic alphabet, 120

Dalmatia, origin of name, 82; necessity for union with north-western Bosnia, 101; character of coast scenery, 198
Derby, Earl of, despatch regarding Bosnian insurrection, 214; speech in 1864, 218, 219
Dervent, 172
Desetina, Government tax of one-tenth of produce, 39

Education, 56—64
England, loss of trade with Bosnia, 109, 110, 265; her past policy in the Balkans, 208—220; what will be her attitude to Macedonia, 266, 277
Eviction of member of a zadruga, or joint family, 41

Freeman, Vice-Consul, report upon Bosnian morality and Mr. Arthur Evan's reply, 74—76

Gacko, 195
Gendarme corps, 15
Ghazis and the punishment accorded to them in India, 23
Gladstone, Right Hon. W. E., speeches, 267, 268
Gornji Šeher, 118
Gradačac, 175

Hobart Pasha, letter urging support of Sultan Abdul Hamid, 216
Horses, Bosnian, powers of endurance, 151

Ilidže, 27
Illyrians, 82
India, system of legal appeals compared with Bosnia, 49; whether it is advisable to have separate tribunals for Mahommedans, 55; strict seclusion of Mahommedan women, 68; survival of caste prejudices amongst forcibly converted Hindu Mahommedans, 132; objection of Mahommedans to engage in trade, or to take interest for money, 158
Irby, Miss, orphanage in Serajevo, 59

Jablanica, 3, 71
Jajce, 129-140
Jews, Spanish, 43

Kara-Vlachi, 171
Kerka, falls of river, 96
Ključ, 146
Kmets, or tenants; tenure by which they hold their land, 39, 40
Koran, exhortation against empty forms of prayer, 34; alms-giving inculcated, 38; denunciation of unfair dealing, 52; women to be veiled, 72; admittance of women to Paradise, 73; injunction to moderation in words and actions, 122; to patience in times of adversity, 123; to be kind to

animals, 154 ; and against usury, 157 ; denunciation of those who defraud, 162 ; and of the infidel 270, 272
Korsakoff, Prince Dondakoff, administration of Eastern Rumelia by, 251
Kossovo, anniversary of battle, 31
Kulenović, Ali Bey, 149

LAND Laws, 38-40
Layard, Sir H., contention that England must be allied with the Turks because Sultan is Caliph of Islam, 224
Law, courts of, 45-58
Luke, St., body where buried, 137

MACEDONIA, liability of women to ill-usage, 79 ; present condition of, 235-237 ; likelihood of revolt ; Policy of Austria and of England, 266-277
Mahommedans, marriage, 64 ; condition of women, 66 ; fatalism, 123 ; customs, 131 ; handicapped in trade by their religion, 161, 162 ; feeling aroused in India by denunciation of the Sultan, 228
Metković, 94
Military frontier, 203-207
Mills, on the Unna, 164 ; on the Save, 183
Mines, in Bosnia under the Romans, 83
Moltke, Baron von, remark concerning Greek war of independence, 260
Montenegro, policy of Austria and of England towards, 198
Mostar, 79, 199

NARENTA, river, 79, 199
Novi, 161

OFFICIALS, Life of Bosnian, 188
Orašje, 176

PETROVAC, 148
Pliva, falls of river, 133
Plums, Bosnian, 184
Population, increase of, 42
Prjedor, 107-112

RADOVA, 22
Ragusa, 197
Railway, forest, 20
Rama, valley of river, 90
Rumelia, Russian administration of Eastern, 251
Russia, policy in the Balkans, 262, 272

SALISBURY, Marquis of, speeches, 209, 219, 270
Salt springs of Tuzla, 184, 185, 272, 276
Šamac, 174
Sandwith, Dr., letters on eastern question, 212, 213, 238
Schools, 56
Scio, massacre of, 240
Sebenico, 96
Serajevo, 18, 32
Serbia, 101, 264, 275
Serbs, 102, 120
Slavonia, 200-203

TRAPPISTS, monastery, 166
Trebinje, 196
Turkey, derivation of name of bird 113, 114
Tuzla, 184

UNNA, river, 164

VAKUF system, 35
Varcar Vakuf, 142

WOMEN, Mahommedan, 66-73, morality of Bosnian, 74-77

ZADRUGA, or joint family, 41
Zupanje, 203

RICHARD CLAY AND SONS, LIMITED
LONDON AND BUNGAY.

www.ingramcontent.com/pod-product-compliance
Lightning Source LLC
Chambersburg PA
CBHW030750230426
43667CB00007B/912